MW00936499

How Imperfect Parents Lead Great Families

Dale and Monica Vernon

Copyright © 2016 Dale and Monica Vernon

All rights reserved. No part of this publication may be reproduced, distributed or transmitted in any form or by any means, including photocopying, recording, or other electronic or mechanical methods, without the prior written permission of the publisher, except in the case of brief quotations embodied in critical reviews and certain other noncommercial uses permitted by copyright law.

For more information, go to www.imperfectparentslead.com

How Imperfect Parents Lead Great Families / Dale and Monica Vernon —1st ed.

ISBN: 9781533250704

Table of Contents

To our many friends who engaged in those philosophical discussions on parenting and life. Thank you for being there for us.

To our friend and partner Mike Coyne we are grateful for your dedication and passion. We could not have done this without you.

To Grant, Elizabeth and Dominic. No one could have prepared us for all it takes to be a parent. Through our journey together we learned the most important thing and that is with Love and Trust anything can be accomplished.

By Monica Vernon

2007-2008 was a tough time in our lives. My husband, Dale, and I were still in transition from our move back to Ohio from Michigan a few years earlier, and we were just getting settled into our new home. Like many families, we talked ourselves into buying a house that stretched our finances. Shortly thereafter, Dale decided on a career change. He left a medical device company and joined a financial services firm, which offered better long-term opportunities. The new job meant a severe pay cut, but he was confident that, with hard work, his income would rise to where it had been, and he would be in a career for which he was better suited.

That fall, I returned to teaching. I cherished the last seven years when I had been a stay-at-home mom, but our youngest child was about to enter kindergarten and the family needed the extra income. Besides, I was ready to get back to the classroom.

As working mothers already know, a career does not exempt one from being a full-time mom and housekeeper. The transition was pretty stressful. I struggled with the increased workload and with missing the kids. I was frequently tired and overwhelmed. Dale struggled with the fact that I was not home all the time to manage everything, and with the reality that he would have to pitch in more if we were going to keep afloat. We often fought and things became pretty chaotic.

One of my biggest concerns at that time was our oldest son's progress in school. In kindergarten and first grade, Grant seemed to be struggling. Even though I knew from my experience as a teacher that some kids take longer than others to adapt to school, he wasn't improving. When his problems continued into the spring of 2008, I started to worry. I was no longer confident that if he kept trying, he would eventually "get it."

For a long time, I was managing these issues on my own. Dale was happy to provide his input – dictating what he thought I should do – but he thought it was my job to manage the problem and deal with it. He rarely participated in the meetings with the school, and didn't fully appreciate that, while I was a good teacher, Grant's problems were well beyond my expertise.

Things really began to unravel in the fall of 2008. Dale was less than one year into his new career when the country entered into what is now known as the "great recession." It was a horrible time for anyone in the financial services business, particularly for someone brand new, whose job was to obtain new clients.

I could see the stress getting to Dale. He had never failed at anything, and whenever something got difficult, his response was to simply work harder. That meant longer hours and less time at home. Unfortunately, this time, working harder was not going to do much in the short-term other than make him more stressed out and irritable.

It was at that time that Grant's problems at school became a crisis. He was falling so far behind that it was becoming difficult for his teachers to help him. We took Grant to see educational specialists, psychologists, and neurologists, all trying to diagnose the cause of his problems and find a way to help him. It took several years to identify all of the obstacles facing him: severe dyslexia, dysgraphia, and attention deficit disorder. He was a virtual melting pot of educational roadblocks.

In December 2008, I insisted that Dale join me in addressing Grant's problems. He did, but with all that was going on, our family wasn't doing well. Dale didn't like dealing with family issues, and he didn't hide his irritation. He had a bad habit of analyzing a problem, dictating a solution, and blaming me when things did not work out the way he thought they should. That angered me and created enormous tension in our home. I'm sure our children felt the stress as well.

My parents had divorced when I was 4 years old. I have a great relationship with both of them, and they did everything they could for me. But I didn't want that for my family. Therefore, I was determined to keep our family together, with Dale's help or not, and despite his behavior.

Fortunately, something miraculous happened. Dale reached his own conclusion that our family was suffering, and decided that it was his job to fix it. More importantly, he concluded that he was the cause of a lot of the problems and had to change. Dale approached this task with the same fanatical work ethic that defines his professional life. He researched and experimented with ways for us to improve communication within our family and to make us more consistent parents. My role in our journey was the same as it has always been in our marriage: to temper and moderate Dale! Together, we made changes in our family that brought us closer together. I believe the experience saved our marriage, saved our family, and saved our son from years of frustration. When I call it miraculous, I'm not exaggerating!

This book is about families and struggles, how to overcome them and come out on top; it is not a story about dyslexia or disabilities. Every family goes through problems and rough times, and, in the end, it's what we do as a family, how we deal with these uncertainties in life, that matters. Our book is about a way that families can deal with the struggles of life through better communication. It offers a way to get where you want to go – wherever that may be.

When Dale was encouraged by a friend to write a book about our story and the communication framework we designed, he asked me to help him write it. I had one requirement: that he tell the story from his perspective. I insisted on this for two reasons. First, since he had driven the change, I thought he could most effectively describe how the changes came about. Second, I knew Dale wouldn't be shy, as I would have been, about sharing some of the more difficult details of our journey.

As Dale shares our story with you, I believe you'll understand why he was the voice of change. It needed to be him. I'm sure you'll also question and wonder what I was feeling and at times even ask, *Why does she put up with him?* Give him, and us, a chance to share our story. Not so you feel empathy or sympathy for us, but so you realize that we are just imperfect parents, maybe just like you. We all have our problems and we all want solutions. We truly believe that the communication framework we've put in place in our family can help your family as well.

I know that some of you reading this book are single or divorced parents. Even though we share our story and communication framework with you as a couple, we do believe that it has a place in every home. We appreciate that the person who will become your sounding board, partner, or support group is not your spouse, but we also realize that we all have *someone*. We'd also like to encourage you to work with your ex to implement some of these strategies, but we know that's not always possible. We can't appreciate all of your struggles, but we are confident that you will find a way to use the communication framework to help your family.

The ideas in this book have allowed our family to thrive, and we hope they will help your family thrive as well.

INTRODUCTION

TV parents are so irritating! They always have the perfect response on the tip of their tongue, even at the most chaotic and dramatic moments. We mortals, on the other hand, find ourselves ending arguments by saying totally ineffective things like, "Because I said so!" and storming around the house demanding to know why no one is listening to our pearls of wisdom. The gift of parenthood is awesome, but the reality of trying to raise good kids while being imperfect parents is frustrating. We all want our children to succeed and we know we have to lead them, but the nagging question of "Are we parenting correctly?" is always there taunting us – and frequently the answer is no. We aren't doing things the best way we could.

Who can blame us? There are, after all, so many decisions facing us in an increasingly complex world. Should we let our kids have smartphones in middle school so they can be part of the social swirl? Should we pour hundreds of hours and dollars into afterschool enrichment activities to boost their chances of success in high school and in life? Should we push them to learn a second language so they can compete in a global society? These are only some of the big questions. There are a million everyday questions too, about how to respond to problems, how to inspire growth, and how to lead our families to happiness.

No one knows what the "right" answers are, and, to make matters worse, we are addressing all these questions and problems in the midst of chaos. In our family, we have two working parents, three busy kids, one demanding dog and, well, you know exactly what that looks like: the average American family. Our usual way of dealing with the frustrations we were having with our children and the chaos of the daily grind – school, work, kids' activities, homework, dinner – was to constantly *react* to outside forces. It prevented us from being in control of our own family.

I'm dyslexic and have ADHD, and it is a wicked combination. I barely made it through high school and only made it to college thanks to wrestling. My dyslexia wasn't diagnosed until I was in college, but, even then, a diagnosis wasn't much help since there were no programs to assist dyslexics at the time. From high school on, my solution to every problem I encountered in life – and there were a lot of problems – was to work three times harder than anyone else, so I could prove that I was worthy. My solution to every problem with my kids was no different: I simply reacted to whatever was happening and assumed that any issue they faced could be solved by getting them to try harder. I had no clue *how* to do that, but it's where I placed all my faith. I was not effectively leading my family, not by a long shot, and I certainly was not raising my children in a thoughtful and deliberate fashion.

Several years ago, Monica and I became acutely aware of our need to "do better" when we faced a crisis with our oldest son, Grant, who was 8 years old and struggling with dyslexia. His problem required a great deal of time, attention, and energy. At times, it left us exhausted and frustrated. It put enormous stress on our family life and a great deal of strain on our marriage. As I will explain in Chapter 1, my misguided attempts to address his problems by trying to build up his confidence created an even greater crisis in our family. Fortunately, it also launched us on the journey that led to this book.

Our path to find a solution – for our son, for ourselves, and for our entire family – was long and difficult. While I figured out that confidence wasn't the singular answer, I learned that there are a lot of ways we can help our kids be happy and successful and make our family life more fulfilling. We used to address family and parenting issues on an ad hoc basis, more often than not with a brief exchange of information and little discussion. We *reacted*. And, in the absence of any other plan, we reacted from that deep, dark place of fear that we simply weren't doing enough or doing things right.

Or, I should say that *I* reacted in that way. My wife, who is a schoolteacher, is far more level-headed than I am, but it was my fear that was driving the bus.

We decided to become intentional about leading our family. We did a lot of reading: books about dyslexia, parenting, confidence, and relationships, anything we thought might make us better parents. We also spent a great deal of time talking about our parenting, our children, and our family. We fought, we haggled, we negotiated, we tried one tactic and then we tried another. Our home became a research laboratory of ideas, strategies, and concepts around family and parenting.

Over time, we developed a simple framework for communicating that led us out of the place of darkness and allowed us to enjoy some success. The framework has three main pillars, which we will share with you in this book:

1. We created *unity* – bringing our family closer together with a shared purpose.
2. We created a culture of communication – bringing greater *clarity* to our conversations with our children and providing all of us with opportunities to learn and grow.
3. We focused on how life's experiences through *action* were an important part of our family's development.

The result of our efforts is that Monica and I are closer, our children are happier, there is less chaos in our home, and we are not letting fear rule our lives.

And our son? You will see in the coming pages how he grew from a frightened, doubtful child into a normal, happy, well-adjusted kid who still sometimes doesn't want to do his homework or clean up his room or face a tough situation, but who does not think of himself as "stupid." The same is true for all our children, who have each faced various challenges inside and outside of school.

We have written this book because we want other parents to shake off the fear that they are not doing enough or are not doing things correctly and enjoy the same benefits that this framework has brought to our family. *How Imperfect Parents Lead Great Families* will provide you with a simple process for exploring who you are, what you believe in, and how to grow together as a family.

HOW IT WORKS – THE THREE PILLARS

Unity

The first and most important step in improving your family life is realizing that change is inevitable and that the only way your family succeeds is when *you* change first. The question you have to ask yourself is, "Am I willing to be a better me, for a better we?" It is by exploring who you are first that you can influence the most significant change and launch the effort to be unified in purpose.

Almost equally important is being sure that you and your spouse are aligned in purpose, because together, you are stronger. We define being aligned as not only sharing similar values, but establishing them by writing them down, declaring them to your family, and integrating them into a common language within your home. Your values provide direction.

Finally, unity means that you routinely gather together as a family and become a family that communicates. It may sound overly formal, but structured meetings with your children are an important way of improving communication and reminding them that they are part of a family that shares values and cares about them.

Clarity

Next, we focus on how to improve communication. Your family values will give your family a common language for talking about everything from who is going to feed the dog to what to do when someone feels bullied. You will notice that your interactions with your children will generally be more positive, more productive, and more intimate, and that is only the beginning. Positive communication with your children involves much more than defining and using your values as a common language. Often, *how* things are said and what you do is as important, or even more important, than *what* is said. We explore six ways to bring clarity to communication between parents and children. Additionally, we show you how to quickly identify and correct those parenting habits that are barriers to effective communication.

Action

The last section of this book discusses action and the role of experience in raising successful children. A child's abilities and confidence can be developed through the process of trying to find solutions and learning from failures. It's not easy to allow our children to fail, but it's crucial. We review the benefits of praising children for their efforts and for the way they approach a task rather than praising them for the results they achieve. You will learn simple and effective ways of encouraging your children to take action: trying new things, taking risks, and focusing on their effort rather than results.

Monica and I continue to be imperfect parents – it's just the nature of the beast – but we have become stronger by coming together to define who we are and what we believe in, developing a common language, and encouraging *all* family members to grow through action. We hope this book will lead you toward the same success.

Unity

Bring Your Family Together

CHAPTER ONE

Together Stronger

Before anything else, agree that a better me is a better we, and go first.

Imperfect Parenting

Parenting is not what I had imagined. It isn't that I don't love my children, but why is it that everything takes 10 times the energy it is supposed to, or at least 10 times what I think it should? And what happened between Monica and me? What happened to those days when we'd been able to go out and just enjoy each other's company? The flame of passion that once burned between us seemed to be no more than a flicker. When we did go out for a rare evening together, we were immersed in conversation about the kids. Usually I spent the evening telling her what she needed to do differently – what she needed to change. I figured that since she was the main caregiver and a stay-at-home mom, whatever wasn't working at home was her responsibility and was probably a consequence of what she wasn't doing right.

It was easy for me to lose myself in my work and forget about the troubles of our home life. It's much easier to focus on things that bring success rather than things that cause struggle. When stuff at home couldn't be ignored, I dealt with it by dictating to, rather than collaborating with, Monica. My attempts to control my family seemed hopeless, and every issue left me exhausted, deflated, and wondering whether I was capable of affecting positive change in our family. Nights like the one back in the fall of 2007, before those fateful words left Grant's mouth, are a good example of how we were heading in the wrong direction.

I was working late at the office – par for the course, if truth be told. Monica called in tears.

"Grant locked himself in his room all afternoon and wouldn't talk to me for hours," she said. "I finally got him to come out and look at me, and all he did was hand me his backpack. Now, he's refusing to do his homework. I need your help."

I was not giving Monica my full attention, as I continued working on the project covering my desk. To be honest, I was annoyed at being disturbed. *Why couldn't she handle this on her own?*

Monica continued to talk about Grant's refusal to do his homework.

"He says he doesn't understand and never will. He just keeps repeating it over and over."

I finally responded,

"Monica, are you kidding me? He's in third grade. That's just him being lazy and not wanting to work hard. Fix this problem."

The next thing I heard was the sound of the phone being slammed down. *Monica just hung up on me,* I thought. *She never does that!*

I was frustrated. I knew that Grant had been struggling at school. Even though he was a third-grader, he was reading at only a first-grade level, at best. In second grade, he'd been tested and found to have severe dyslexia. As with most dyslexics, this meant that reading and comprehension were more difficult for him, but it had nothing to do with his innate intelligence. (Unfortunately, his dyslexia was far more severe than we appreciated, and far more severe than mine.) I found myself getting angry – at Grant. I was convinced that his problem was mostly simple laziness. In my mind, being dyslexic simply meant you had to work harder than everyone else. That was, after all, what I had done.

Monica and I had fought for years about Grant's reading. It felt like I had told her a thousand times to spend more time reading with him and that it would solve the problem. Of course, I had no idea of the substantial amount of time that she *was* spending with him. She had been home with him and the other kids for seven years before returning to her professional career as a teacher. I thought, *She's a teacher for God's sake. Why can't she manage this?* Grant just needed to work harder, and Monica needed to stop babying him. His future was at stake, and she wanted to coddle him instead of push him.

When I walked in the door an hour after Monica had hung up on me, the two younger kids were down in the basement playing. Grant was sitting at the kitchen table in front of a tear-splattered story and a page of reading comprehension questions. Monica was sitting next to him, working on her lesson plan for her own classroom, and assisting and encouraging Grant. Even though she didn't look up to acknowledge me, I could feel her steely resolve. She'd been at this for hours, had work to do, and was at her wit's end.

"Hey, Buddy," I said to Grant.

"I hate reading," he said. "I hate school, too! I can't do this."

"He says Mrs. Armstrong thinks he's stupid," Monica commented.

"She *does*," Grant yelled. "She called me stupid!"

"Grant," I said. "Your teacher didn't call you stupid. You've got to take responsibility, get focused, and get your homework done."

I saw Monica roll her eyes, but, as with her earlier silence, I didn't stop to think what it meant.

"I'm going in tomorrow after school," she said. "You need to come with me."

I had back-to-back meetings planned, an important presentation, and a big meeting with a prospective client.

As if I had already objected, Monica said, "You need to come, Dale."

"I can't," I replied. "I have a meeting. Remember, someone has to provide for this family. You need to deal with this." I turned around and stormed off to my home office.

There was so much darkness in our home that night. Grant thought his teacher had called him stupid, and he thought *we* weren't listening to him. He had no framework for making positive change, because we hadn't given it to him. Monica thought I wasn't listening to her or to Grant. She thought I parented the way I ran my business life – as a manager who expected results – and she was exhausted and terrified about what would happen to Grant. I knew we both were worried that cracks were appearing in our marriage and our family.

I was irritated that my family couldn't follow my instructions about taking responsibility and doing their jobs. I was disappointed in Monica for not handling what I assumed her professional training would have prepared her for, and angry for being dragged into something that would take away from my *real* work, where, even on the worst days, I had some sense of control.

In other words, we were imperfect parents running an imperfect family and we were leading it into the ground – with me at the helm.

It all came to a head one awful night at the end of Christmas vacation when I went to say goodnight to Grant.

"Dad, I don't want to go back to school," he said.

As a perfectly imperfect parent, I reacted to the situation without stopping to think. I assumed I knew what the problem was and did not take the time to stop and ask why.

I simply said, "Don't worry. After a couple days you'll get back into the swing of things."

My son's response changed everything. Grant looked at me and, calmly and without emotion, said, "No Dad, you don't get it. I'm the stupid kid."

His words left me speechless. I could tell by the look in his eyes that he really believed what he was telling me.

I felt like someone had thrown me to the ground and was standing on my chest. How had we failed Grant so badly? I knew then that I could no longer sit back and wait for something to change. I was beginning to realize that I was a big part of the problem, and I had to change how I was parenting.

But how? I was convinced that if I built up Grant's confidence, it would not only be the answer to his problems, but it would put our whole family in a better place as well. It had worked for me. I was a good wrestler my first couple of years in college, but I wasn't great. What was missing, however, wasn't my ability, but my *belief* in my ability. Entering my junior year of college, I started to believe in my ability. When I found my confidence, it launched my success and led me to achieve All-American status – and it didn't stop there. Once I knew what confidence looked like, I learned how to use it in all areas of life, right up to my professional career. I knew what Grant needed was to believe in himself and develop confidence, and I was certain that what had been true for me would be true for Grant: With confidence, he could succeed at anything.

The trouble was that, while I knew how to build confidence in myself, I just wasn't sure how to instill it in an 8-year-old. I tackled this problem like I tackled most problems in life: I fully immersed myself in learning everything I could. I was determined to find answers, and I spent endless hours reading books and articles and searching the Internet to learn about building confidence in children. It was frustrating. There appeared to be an endless stream of information and opinion about "what" the problems were and "what" caused them, but I was still missing the "how" – how do we fix our particular problem? How do we *do* it? Ultimately, I decided that if we continuously told Grant to believe in himself, he would get the message. He would get through this rough spot, become confident, and get back into the swing of things at school.

At every opportunity, I gave a mini lecture about what I had learned: "Believe in yourself, take responsibility, and take action – take that first step." It became a mantra that no matter what was going on with our kids, I would repeat: "Believe in yourself, take responsibility, and take action – take that first step." I repeated this lecture often, because it felt like the right thing to do to build the confidence that all of our children needed. I was convinced that the more they heard it, the more likely they were to put it into action.

While I was pushing forward with my focus on confidence Monica needed to complete her master's degree to retain her teacher's license and chose to focus on reading education to better understand how she could help Grant. During this time we were both arming ourselves with plenty of "what" but we still lacked the "how." This continued from Grant's 3rd through 4th grade years. We never really talked about how or whether our different "solutions" to Grant's problems fit together, or whether our approaches were even working. We just plowed ahead separately

In addition to our individual efforts, we also sought specialized help for Grant. We realized that his dyslexia was a bigger problem than we could handle alone, so we sought advice from specialists, physicians, and other educators – only to learn that, while dyslexia is now a well-known condition, it is hard to find educational institutions with the resources to help dyslexic students.

It quickly became obvious to us that Grant's school didn't understand the extent of his dyslexia and didn't have the resources to manage it, so we looked for a new school. Several schools, when asked directly if they could help Grant, turned us away, saying, "This isn't the place for him." We were grateful for their honesty.

By the end of Grant's third grade year, we were able to find a school that did have the resources. It was an hour away from our home, but at that point we were willing to try anything. We enrolled Grant and took on the brutal commute for the next three years.

The new school seemed to help, but it always felt like we were treading water and not really making the long-term progress Grant needed. Our family life was still chaotic. Monica continued to work with Grant and tried to comfort and console him when his frustration erupted in an emotional outburst. Monica clearly shared his frustration. Many nights, Grant fell asleep in Monica's arms, while she gently wept over his suffering and our inability to help him. We still had no real idea how to do anything other than stumble from one day to the next, and all I was doing differently was repeating my mantra. Grant had trouble making friends at a school so far away from home, and our time dedicated to going back and forth, and seeing tutors and specialists, kept the entire family from living a "normal" life.

The true nature of our tenuous hold on our family life came one day as I was giving my "take responsibility, take action" lecture to the kids. Suddenly Monica snapped.

"Dale, stop! You're scaring the kids!"

Huh?

Turns out the kids had been literally avoiding me because they knew what I was going to say no matter what the problem was: late homework, a room not picked up, chores not done. I was going to step onto my soapbox and begin "the lecture." I was so far from listening to them, being engaged with them, or teaching or leading them – and in that moment, I suddenly knew it.

So I did what so many of us do when our weaknesses are called out: I shot back at my spouse.

"The problem, Monica," I said, "is that you're not reinforcing the message." In other words, it wasn't me, it was her.

Although I made that comment with authority, I really did know better. *My kids were afraid of me? No more.* It was time to make a profound change. I realized that all my research had taught me were ways to think about the importance of confidence, which was great information but still wasn't the answer. Besides, I did not have a clue how to put it all together in practice with my family. I had no clue *how* to make the changes we needed, except to just try to piece ideas together and give them a whirl.

Feelings of depression started to set in. I started to question my own thinking and my effectiveness. *Why couldn't I lead my family? What was wrong with me?* I looked in the mirror many times and asked myself, "Who are you?" I wanted to blame Monica, but deep down I knew she wasn't the problem. I knew exactly who was.

I spent a great deal of time reflecting and praying for help, direction, *something*. I spent even more time talking to friends about what was going on with me and my family. Through all of these conversations, I came to the realization that the thing that needed to change was the thing I had the most control of: me. I loved my children, I loved Monica, and if there was something worth changing for, it was my family. I was resolved, but I didn't know where to start.

Around the time this was occurring, I was becoming friends with Patrick, who also worked in the financial services industry. He lived near me, and we engaged in many discussions about life and family. Patrick had been the poster boy for a hard-working executive, working long hours, frequently on the road and away from home. All of that had changed a few years earlier when he was diagnosed with cancer and chose to have his arm amputated to save his life. Since that time, he had become a different person, and he really seemed to have control of things.

As we sat on my patio under the stars with a drink in hand, I shared my struggles with him. He told me that when he realized he needed to change, he went to his wife and asked her a tough question: "How do you see me as a father and how do you see me as a husband?" He asked his wife to open up about the kind of feelings that spouses usually keep to themselves.

"It was an eye-opening experience, Dale," he said. "I heard things that I didn't expect, and things I didn't want to hear but needed to. That was the beginning for me. I changed my priorities and my focus, and now I couldn't be happier."

I was moved by his courage and mindful of how similar we were in our struggle for work-life balance. I started to think that maybe I should ask Monica the same question, but, like most things, it was easier said than done. I spent several weeks thinking about how to approach it. I reflected on who I thought I was, what I did well as a father and husband, and what I didn't. Finally, after about a month, I worked up the courage to ask Monica to sit down and talk.

Monica never knows what to expect when I ask for one of these sit-downs, but she knows that deep conversations are my modus operandi. Still, I was certain she didn't see what was coming that evening. As soon as she sat down, I began.

"Monica, I know we are not doing well, and I now realize what the problem is."

Monica looked up and made eye contact, almost as if to say, *You'd better not start telling me I'm the problem and what I need to change, again!*

I continued without pause, "*I'm* what needs to change."

That caught her attention and I saw her posture relax.

"I want to share with you who I think I am and what I believe I need to change. When I'm finished, I need you to tell me what you think of me as a father and husband."

I paused for a response. I didn't get one, so I asked, "Can we do that?"

I could tell Monica was uncomfortable with the request. After a long pause, she slowly responded, "Sure."

I acknowledged that my focus had been on work and not the family and helping her, that I did not control my temper as I should, that I did not do a very good job of trying to understand how I could help her with what was going on at home. Instead, I assumed that I understood what the problem was and assumed I knew how it could be fixed – often without my direct involvement. I went on for another 15 minutes before I asked Monica to share her thoughts.

Monica sat quietly as she collected her thoughts. I tried to be patient, but patience isn't natural for someone with a type A personality and ADHD. Finally, I spoke again.

"Monica, I need to know what you are thinking."

She began to speak, softly and slowly.

"It's hard to tell someone you love something negative," she said.

I paused a moment before responding.

"I know, but this is what we have to do in order to help our family. It's not about you and me, it's about our family."

That was enough. Monica nodded and then let it fly.

She told me that I worked too much. I was disengaged, and wasn't home even when I was at home. My habit of working in my home office after dinner created the impression that I didn't care about my family – only about work – and the kids thought that too. She told me that I was dictatorial, that I tried to run the house like I ran my business, and that kids don't always have to be focused on improving something. She reminded me that she and the kids were family, not employees.

Our conversation went on for another hour. It was painful, eye-opening, and one of the best conversations of our marriage. I would have paid anything to just be imperfect; instead I was hearing about a person that I didn't even like. I had no idea of the extent to which my behavior was harming my family and the extent to which the kids saw it. I started to feel sick about the person she was describing. I wanted to resist. *That can't be me,* I thought, but it was obvious that it was, so I resisted the urge to defend myself.

For the next several days I walked around with Monica's criticisms in my head, feeling as though I had been stripped of all my skin. It felt pretty awful. She had described a person I simply hadn't seen, and someone I wouldn't like if I met him on the golf course, at a neighborhood barbecue, or at church. It wasn't the person I wanted to be or who I thought I was. From time to time, I would try to tell myself that I wasn't as bad as Monica described, but I knew better. She hadn't spoken out of anger but out of love.

I realized that if we could have an open, honest conversation like that, with nothing to hide and with a focus on improving ourselves for the benefit of our family, we could get our marriage, our family, and our children to a place where we all needed to be to succeed. The focus was now about "a better me for a better we."

I spent the next several weeks working through our conversation and paying more attention to my behavior. As I worked to improve, the guilt I had been feeling was gradually replaced by a genuine enthusiasm for making change, not only in myself but in our family.

I wanted Monica to know what I had learned from our conversation, and I wanted to take the process one step farther. I approached her cautiously.

"Monica, we need to have the same conversation about you that we had about me."

She looked at me and said, "I know. I knew that was coming."

I guess after 13 years of marriage and 21 years after we started dating, I had become a bit predictable. She quickly agreed to have the conversation, which was brave of her. I had asked for the criticism – she had not.

I told Monica that she was disorganized, always reacting instead of planning. In my judgment, she needed to be more consistent with the kids, more purposeful. I was trying to be objective, and I believe I was, but she could have easily heard my critique as telling her that she should be more like me.

I suppose things could have gone either way at that time. We could have let our marriage and our family die on the vine, choked off by the pain of the truth. But we were in too deep. We knew that we were married for a reason. We grew up with similar values and believed in the importance of family. We reminded each other that the tough conversations we were having were for the love of each other and our family. Consequently, rather than push us apart, these conversations drew us closer together. Monica later told me that while she was angry at my initial critique, she chose to not react because she knew I was trying to make things better. Thank God for her patience!

Over the next couple of months, we continued our talks, but gradually the tone changed. It became less about pointing out each other's faults and more about sharing our fears and concerns. We speculated as to what the kids thought of us – did they view us as competing forces in their lives, or did they see us as one? Did they realize we were learning as we went and were making mistakes along the way? Did we create an environment where they were comfortable to talk to us about anything? Were we creating the right culture in our home for their happiness and success? We also discussed each one of them, their personalities, their strengths and weaknesses, and where our developmental focus should be with each of them.

We started asking ourselves what we thought "family" meant to our kids and what we *wanted* it to mean to them, what we believed in as a family, and how we wanted to live our lives. There was a pretty big gap between those ideas. We asked ourselves what we could do better to lead our family, and it was from that point that we began to make changes that would have a profound and lasting impact. The realization of "a better me for a better we" was what we needed. As we communicated and became aligned as parents, we realized that together we were stronger for each other and for our family.

Purpose Not Perfection

Dealing with challenges is part of life. The challenges that our family has faced are no different than the problems faced by many families. Indeed, many families have much greater problems. Each day, we are presented with issues and circumstances that we must manage. How we deal with these issues and circumstances is what is critical. If we are not engaged in addressing family problems, there is a good likelihood that we are making things worse.

When faced with marriage or family problems, it is human nature to focus on the faults of others instead of our own. It's easier to look at others as the problem and say, "It's them, not me." *Attitude*, the famous poem by Charles Swindoll, says, "Life is 10% what happens to me and 90% how I react to it." Yet, it seems like we spend 90% of the time looking at others as the problem and 10% of the time looking at ourselves. Your willingness to take a deep look at yourself and be your biggest critic is the key to having a successful marriage and successful family.

It's not easy, but you must be willing to begin a process of self-evaluation and reflection. Ask yourself the difficult questions: *Who am I? Am I the person I want to be? Am I the person my family needs me to be?* This is the starting point to becoming a better me for the one thing that matters most in life: your family.

One of life's cruel realities is that we are imperfect. Frequently, we look at our spouse and expect perfection, yet we ourselves are not providing it. Being imperfect is a fact of life. We can't expect of others what we ourselves can't deliver. If perfection is your objective as a parent, you will have a lifetime of disappointment. Your time and energy is better spent where it can make a real difference – purpose not perfection.

You are not alone on this journey. Feedback from a spouse, parent, or close friend is critical to helping you understand who you are and how you can improve. When you are willing to open yourself up to feedback, you open the door for conversations about your parenting and your family. Open, honest conversations are not easy, but they are a critical step in creating a culture of communication in your home.

When I asked Monica to tell me what kind of father I was, she said, "It's hard to tell someone you love something negative." This was a critical step. She was reminding me about her love for me before giving me her critique. Reminding each other of your love, your own imperfections, and your desire to see each other and your family succeed is a great way to come together.

We always tell our children to try to put forth effort, whether they succeed or not. The experience is just as valuable as success. If you and your spouse know that you are putting forth the effort and trying to improve, you will find a great deal of happiness in your relationship, even as imperfect spouses and parents. If you are reading this book, it is because you have a desire to do the best for your children and your family. If you and your spouse are ready to open yourselves up to each other in order to become a better me, then you've started the journey. Be the change you want to see in your family.

Together Stronger

A better me for a better we

It begins with the realization and courage to make changes where they will have the most impact ... with yourself.

Go first. We may think it's the other person, but someone must go first. Remember, it's for a better we: your family.

Spend time in reflection

Am I the person I want to be?

Am I the parent/spouse/partner I want to be?

What is the example I'm setting for my kids/family?

What am I willing to do and how far am I willing to go for my family?

What is it that I really want for my family?

Together stronger

Sit down with your spouse, partner, family member, or friend who knows you best and tell them what you want to achieve.

Share with them who you think you are.

Ask them who they think you are.

Listen, ask clarifying questions – don't defend yourself, just listen and learn.

Reflect on the feedback

Take the time to reflect, several times, on what you heard. Once the sting of hearing a new reality goes away, you will find opportunity for self-improvement.

Make a list of what you want to improve; start with one thing and get started today.

Meet again, keep talking, continue to reflect

Ongoing conversations and open communication will help your development.

Be aware and forgiving

Don't be hard on yourself. This isn't about guilt, but development.

This is a journey and it will take time. Nothing happens quickly.

CHAPTER TWO

Declare Your Values

Define what you believe in through your family values.

Imperfect Parenting

Monica and I continued our conversation about our family over the next several months, and it felt like we were growing closer, much like we were when we were newlyweds. While we were making progress in understanding each other and ourselves, we also were beginning to find a way to face our family's challenges together. I think part of it was that we were talking about our family in a way that was aspirational. We weren't looking to find fault with each other so much as we were looking for ways to overcome our common imperfections.

Still, amid these discussions, we continued to feel overwhelmed by the pace and pressure of daily life. Just talking about helping our family wasn't bringing about the change we needed.

One day, on the 35-minute drive from work, I found myself asking, *What is it about families and businesses that make them successful?* In the professional world, all of the companies I've read about and have seen firsthand have something specific at their heart that you could name and share. Steve Jobs established it at Apple. Richard Branson established it at Virgin Airlines. It's something that becomes part of the DNA of the company, part of the culture. Simply put, these companies KNOW WHO THEY ARE.

For me, this was an epiphany, and I couldn't wait until the next time Monica and I sat down to talk – and I mean I really *couldn't wait*: I threw it at her immediately when I came home from the office that evening.

"Monica," I said, "we need a mission statement for our family."

Monica looked up from her schoolwork and stared at me quizzically.

"What are you talking about?"

I frenetically explained to her my revelation that our discussions over the last several weeks had left out anything *actionable*. We weren't *doing* anything to help us define who we were as a family or putting our ideas into practice. I thought for a moment about using a business example, but doing so with Monica usually causes an immediate wall to go up. She is not a businessperson. She is a professional teacher and a mother. She doesn't think in terms of business the way I do. So I came up with a different analogy.

"We need a flight plan," I said. "You can't start a journey without knowing where you are going and how you are going to get there." Of course, to me, my idea was pure genius, and I couldn't imagine that Monica wasn't going to immediately agree.

Monica took a deep breath.

"Dale," she said, "our kids haven't even reached middle school yet. How are they going to understand a mission statement? And as I've told you before, we are a family, not a business. Talking about our family as if it is a business takes the joy out of being a mom. Let's just be a family."

Fair enough. If talking about our family in business terms was going to ruin our momentum that was enough reason to stop. Besides, after thinking about it, I realized I have never been that big a fan of mission statements. There always seems to be a lot of energy and passion while the mission statement is being developed, but once it is printed and hung on the wall, everyone seems to forget about it.

What really mattered to me was making sure that Monica and I could articulate the values that we share and want to pass on to our children. I felt that if we could do that, we would be well on our way to stopping the chaotic rush of family life. After all, it was shared values that brought us together in the first place.

Monica and I started dating when we were 17. We were both raised as Catholics in the Midwest in middle-class families, and we share a lot of the same beliefs and values. That's probably a big reason why we were attracted to each other and decided to build a life together.

But we had never actually sat down and discussed who we were and what we believed in. We'd never articulated it, and if we couldn't do that, how could we communicate our values to our children?

I don't know whether my parents ever sat down and discussed the values that they wanted to teach me and my siblings, but I remember hearing a lot of stories from them, and from my grandparents, that spoke to the need to be honest, hard-working, and the like. Family dinners were frequent and dinners with my grandparents were standard every weekend. I think it's fair to say that a few decades ago, families spent more time together, if for no other reason than there weren't that many alternatives available on weekends. There was little in the way of video games, no social media, and far fewer organized kids' activities. We are up against far tougher competition today. If we are not intentional about communicating our values, then our children could easily adopt values that are not what we believe in.

I came back to Monica and said to her, "You're right. The mission statement is a stupid idea. But we do need to talk about our values and what values we want to emphasize with the kids."

Monica agreed.

"Okay, no more missionizing," she said, making up a new verb. "Let's just focus on the kids." She would go on to use that made-up word to tease me for years to come.

We decided to make a list of the values that we believed in and wanted to teach our children. Both of us made a list, and then we compared them. I think it was comforting for us to see a lot of overlap – we really did believe in the same things. But our combined list was really long: about 30 different values! It seemed that we believed in too much. The whole purpose of identifying our shared values was to communicate them to our kids, so clearly we had to narrow down the list to the key values that provided the foundation of our beliefs. We had to shorten it.

Monica said that, given their ages, our children could process and comprehend about six items. I remember her saying, "Less would be better, but no more than six."

I thought cutting down our list was going to be a quick and easy process, but it wasn't. It was actually very frustrating. There are so many values that I believe should define our family, including kindness, faithfulness, and self-discipline. Even today, when someone else shares their family values with us, I find myself thinking, *Darn! That should be one of ours!* However, Monica was right. We needed to keep the list of values short and simple, because that would allow us to make it actionable for the kids and for the family as a whole.

Over several weeks, we developed a combined list of six Vernon Family Values. They were:

- ✓ Honesty
- ✓ Loyalty
- ✓ Leadership
- ✓ Respect
- ✓ Integrity
- ✓ Courage

Interestingly enough, after we cut down the list, we continued to define who we were and what we believed in. We ended up changing loyalty to positivity, because we felt that our family needed to focus on positive energy – being positive and finding the positive in ourselves and in others. The final list became:

- ✓ Honesty- to ourselves and to others
- ✓ Positiveness- in ourselves, in everyone, and in everything
- ✓ Leadership- lead by our actions, be a positive influence on others
- ✓ Respect- the Golden Rule: treat others how we want to be treated
- ✓ Integrity - our words and actions match
- ✓ Courage- stand up for what is right and just

Once we identified the values that we wanted to teach our children, we were clearly on the same page and prepared to develop a family culture built around these values. The values were something we could take action with, discuss, and share with our children.

How? When we ask our kids to do something, we can point to one of the values as the reason for asking. For example, if we want them to quit fighting, we can point to the importance of having respect for each other and approaching each other with honesty. If we ask them to do something difficult, we can point to the importance of courage. We'll discuss this more later, but, for us, parenting in the context of values became much more effective than saying, "Because I said so."

Purpose Not Perfection

Shared values help define a culture. Culture is not typically a term we hear regarding family; it is more commonly used in the context of societies, businesses, and sometimes sports teams, but families do have a culture. In this sense, "family culture" means how we are going to live our lives, what we believe in, and how we do things. Our values help us define what is important in our lives. They are the principles that guide our behavior and decision-making. The values that you cultivate in your family, and how you live those values, define your family culture.

Having consistent and articulated core values will give your children the framework for responding to life's challenges and for making good decisions. Core values provide your child with focus and direction. For example, if your children grow up knowing the importance of truthfulness and the value placed on it, they will be much more likely to be truthful when faced with a difficult situation. It is fair to say that your family's values will help define your child's character throughout his or her life.

Whether it is intentional or not, you are instilling values in your children today that will be reflected in their decision-making for the rest of their lives. Children learn our values from not only things we say, but how we behave and how we react to various situations. Without focus and intention, some of our vices could be mistakenly perceived by our children as a value or a virtue. For example, if you want your children to have a positive attitude, but they hear you constantly complaining, then they are far more likely to be complainers themselves.

Declaring your family's values is an important step in creating a family culture. When you and your partner share the same values and speak with one voice, it is far more likely that your children will accept your values as their own, because the lessons you teach will be consistent, continuous, and in a common language that your children will learn to understand.

In future chapters, you will see how your declared values provide an important part of the framework for communicating with your children. Your children will come to learn that much of what is asked of them is not because of your whim or for your convenience, but because of your allegiance to your family's shared values.

An additional advantage of declaring values and creating an intentional family culture is that it helps your children realize that they are part of something much bigger than themselves. Having values and purpose will give your family happiness and fulfillment, because your focus and direction are clear.

Declare Your Values

Sit down and define

What do you want for your family?

What do you believe in and want your children to believe in?

What kind of person do you want your children to become?

What do you need to teach your children?

List of values

Start a list of values that resonate with you.

Group the values into common themes and meanings. It will help you narrow down your list.

Narrow the list of values

Discuss your list of values. Discuss what each one means to you and why you think it represents your family and what you believe.

Pick the best (6-10) values that you want to define your family.

Define your values

Create simple, age-appropriate definitions for each value.

Declare your values

Prepare to share them when you gather together.

CHAPTER THREE

Gather Together

Establish your family's culture of communication by bringing your family together.

Imperfect Parenting

The several months that Monica and I spent coming together and developing a set of values brought us closer together, but it was only the first step to improving our family life. We were anxious to share these values with our children in a focused way as quickly as possible, but we had trouble finding the time. We thought a family dinner might be the perfect opportunity.

Experts often suggest that family dinners are a powerful time to connect, and they can be. They allow the family to sit together, to talk about their day, to share their problems and their joys. This is a great idea in theory, but, in practice, it was difficult for us. My work involves unavoidable dinners and evening meetings with clients. I am absent from home at least one or two nights, almost every week. Even if I'm home, Monica's work and the children's activities sometimes prevent us from sitting down for dinner as a family. Monica and I are committed to having family dinners as often as possible, but we seem to pull it off only a few nights a week.

It was at one of these dinners that we tried talking to the kids about family values. Monica started.

"Kids, I want you to listen up for a few minutes. We're going to have a discussion concerning our family values."

Dominic, the youngest child, immediately asked, "What are values?" Dominic is eager to ask questions about anything, from the moment he wakes up until he closes his eyes at night, so we should have seen that coming. We realized that our discussion of family values was not going to be a simple task.

"Well," I said, "values are what we believe in, the rules that you try to live your life by." While I was talking and scrambling in my head to come up with a simple explanation, I was looking desperately across the table at Monica for some help. I was hoping she would draw on all her years as a teacher and help me simplify the message. I could tell by the smirk on her face, however, that she was amused by my uncharacteristic loss for words. I still believed that coming together as a family was a simple, easy task, and she knew the truth: that it would be a long, complicated journey.

"I don't get it," Dominic responded.

Monica thankfully came to the rescue.

"A value is something that is important to us, like rules that we want to follow and live by," she said. "For example, a value would be to treat people the way you want to be treated. How does it make you feel when Elizabeth makes fun of you for not getting past a certain level on Angry Birds?"

"Mad," Dominic replied.

"Exactly," Monica said. "So, one of your values would be to not use words that are going to hurt someone's feelings – or, in other words, to 'treat people the way you want to be treated.'"

"Okay, that makes sense," he said.

Dominic's older sister, Elizabeth, chimed in.

"I believe that Dominic is a dingis, but I know that is not a value. Do we have to talk about this?"

I cringed inside. Elizabeth had just done exactly the opposite of what we had discussed. It felt willful and disrespectful. It was one more sign that we were not doing as good a job as a family as we could.

"Look," I said, "Mom and I worked together to come up with a list of our family values. Let's start with an easy one: respect. Respect means treating people how you want to be treated. It is known as the Golden Rule. Elizabeth, you called your brother a dingis. Do you want to be called a dingis?"

"Nope, because I'm not one – but Dominic is."

As I struggled to keep from losing my temper, Monica turned toward Elizabeth.

"What about when someone calls you a name that you don't like? How does that make you feel?"

Elizabeth, perhaps realizing she wasn't going to win this argument, replied, "Not good."

"Well, then you shouldn't call people names, either. You should treat them the way you want to be treated."

Elizabeth, mimicking a character in one of her favorite TV shows, looked at Monica, stuck up her thumb, and said, "You got it, dude."

With that lesson taken care of, I figured it was back to my turn.

"Another family value is being honest to ourselves and to others," I said.

Grant decided it was his turn to speak up.

"Do we have to memorize them? I hate memorizing!"

"It's really not about memorizing," I said. "It's about learning what these values mean, understanding that they are important to the family, and using these values when we make decisions."

The glazed look in Grant's eyes informed me that he was not planning on putting too much focus on this important topic. And then Elizabeth said, "What's for dessert?"

I looked over at Monica, and she raised her eyebrows with a look that said sarcastically, *Well, this is going well.*

We needed to come up with a plan B. We needed a better way to connect as a family on a regular and consistent basis, and a forum for discussing important topics.

I began searching the Web for more information on family improvement and came across the term "family meeting." As I continued my online search, I found a great deal of material on other families that struggled with the same day-to-day chaos with which we were struggling. The parents wrote about how they formalized processes to better keep in touch with each other and to increase opportunities for meaningful interaction with their kids. Perhaps family meetings were the answer.

That got me jacked up. If there's anything I know how to do, it's how to run a meeting. It's a daily ritual for me in my professional life, and I pride myself in being short, efficient, and productive. In my mind, these meetings would be the perfect opportunity to discuss family values with the kids.

When I broached the subject with Monica, she was hesitant.

"Dale, I just don't know if the kids are ready for formal meetings."

I promised Monica that the meetings would be short and well organized, and so she agreed to give it a try. But I thought, *Honesty is a family value, and I'm probably only being half honest with my wife.* I would be sure that the meetings were well organized, but I couldn't imagine that they would be short – we simply had too many things to discuss. We set a meeting time for the following Sunday night, and Monica and I met first to go over the agenda.

As predicted, our first meeting was way too long. Monica remembers it lasting several hours. I don't think it was that long, but it certainly was too long. The agenda I prepared would have filled a good four-hour strategic planning session. Topics: Meeting Rules, Family Values, Week in Review and Observations from Past Week,

Education Update, Miscellaneous. The first meeting did not allow for much participation, as I did most of the talking. I chalked that up to the fact that it was a new experience for the family. When we finally adjourned, it was pretty clear that I had lost my audience.

The next day, after the kids were in bed, Monica and I sat down with a glass of wine for a debriefing.

"So, how do you think our family meeting went?"

"Dale? Are you kidding me? You were the only one who talked. It reminded me of being back in college where a professor lectures and every now and then a debate breaks out. Regardless, eventually the professor resolves the debate and the agenda gets pushed forward. If that is what your team at the office has to deal with, then I really feel sorry for them!"

I felt stung. I hadn't thought it was THAT bad.

"Is that how the kids felt?" I asked.

"Not exactly," Monica replied. "Liz thought it was boring, and Dominic said it was creepy."

"Creepy?"

"He's only 8. He's not used to attending meetings and he couldn't grasp what it was all about. You and I can call our family meetings 'meetings,' but we have to describe them to the kids in a language they understand. They need to be kid-friendly."

During the next few weeks, we continued to meet on Sundays at 6 p.m. We would start each meeting by reciting the six family values: honesty, positiveness, leadership, respect, integrity, and courage. I modified the content and tried to tone down the formality of our family meetings, but they still did not go well. We were lucky if we could keep the kids' attention for more than 10 minutes, after which they would stop sitting still and start asking, "Are we done yet?"

I asked Monica what she thought was wrong.

"Dale, you need to view the meetings from our kids' perspective. They are parent-focused, agenda-driven, repetitive, and dictatorial.

You – we – make the agenda about what we want to talk about. We haven't even asked them what they would like to talk about."

I had to concede that my approach was not working. It was clear that coming to a family meeting with a full agenda of family matters to discuss might not be possible. We agreed that we had to find a way to get the kids to buy into the meetings.

Toward that end, we tried almost everything. We had one meeting that involved each member of the family giving a compliment to every other member of the family. It started slowly.

Elizabeth said, "Dominic did a good job of cleaning up the kitchen."

Then Grant piped up. "Elizabeth helped me clean the basement and I didn't even ask her."

Over time, the kids really embraced this part of the meeting. I liked it, too, because it became an opportunity for Monica and me to learn of positive things going on in our family that we didn't always see. It seemed as though the kids liked supporting each other to make us aware that there were a lot of positive things happening.

Sometimes, we used the meetings to discuss vacations and family outings. We found what ultimately worked was to start with asking the kids what they wanted to discuss and at times letting them lead the entire meeting. Over the years, the kids realized this was the place to have things discussed that were important to them; they slowly began to buy in.

I asked Monica on multiple occasions whether she felt the meetings were helpful. She said they were, but she wasn't selling her enthusiasm and I wasn't buying her less-than-compelling responses. Without enthusiasm from both of us, I feared we would lose momentum – and we did. During the summer that first year, we seemed to miss more meetings than we held. In July, after having gone four weeks in a row without a meeting, the family came together one Sunday and I have to admit that I didn't have much hope for our fledgling effort.

Monica started off the meeting with a rhetorical question, and, much to my surprise, that became our breakthrough moment.

"Do you realize that we are not as good a family when we don't meet?" she asked.

Wow! It was a good thing I wasn't playing poker at that moment, because it would have been obvious I was sitting on a Royal Flush. In the weeks since we had stopped meeting, Monica had truly bought into the need for our family meetings! She had been frustrated with how the kids had been acting and handling things over the summer, and she let them know it.

She went on to say that we were disorganized and not acting like a family that cared about each other. Monica continued giving examples, and, true to her teacher form, gracefully morphed from a lecture to a lesson.

"We've had fun this summer, we've done some fun things, and one important thing we had been doing has fallen by the wayside," she said. "I didn't realize how important these family meeting were until we stopped having them as often."

"Hmmm Mom, I kind of agree with you," Elizabeth chimed in.

Monica quickly continued, "We have a camping trip coming up. I – I mean, your father and I – need to see you kids and us as a family pulling together more. You haven't really been treating each other in a manner you want to be treated ... you know, with respect, the Golden Rule – a family value. You get kind of goofy and fool around with each other, and I feel you've taken it too far."

As she spoke, my eyes opened to the realization that the wrong person had been driving the meetings. Monica could bring the "teacher's touch" to our meetings, making them less formal, more fun, and more engaging for the children.

We shifted so that she would take the lead, and soon we got back to our regular schedule of weekly meetings.

Sometimes we read books together as a family and discussed them at our meetings. The first book we read was William Bennett's *The Children's Book of Virtues*. This allowed us to discuss important topics like courage, perseverance, dreaming, compassion, faith, and so much more. The kids would team up together to read a book and present the values it highlighted to Monica and me in the meetings. Dr. Seuss books where pretty common, too – *Horton Hears a Who, Horton Hatches the Egg, How the Grinch Stole Christmas* – and the kids enjoyed discussing them. Grant and Elizabeth usually teamed up together, but our Little Napoleon, Dominic, wanted to tackle books all on his own. Eventually, all three would read together and come up with a list of ideas to share. They did this as a team, and we were happy to see them working together to achieve a task.

At other times, we would identify a problem that the family or a member the family was facing and use the meeting as an exercise in problem-solving. Sometimes we would simply discuss something that happened at school or in the news. The key was that we were talking as a family and were more aware of what was going on, both in each other's lives and in the world.

Among the topics were Grant's problems at school. They did not dominate the discussion, but they came up from time to time, as one of many things we talked about, and I think this served to normalize the problems for Grant. He began to see them as just one of the many problems that people have to overcome.

I vividly remember one particular conversation regarding the tragic shooting at Sandy Hook Elementary School in 2012. The kids had learned about the shooting at school, and they had talked about it at school that day. They were frightened – as were we – and I felt so blessed that we had a process in place to discuss a troubling event such as that.

As happy as I had become with family meetings, I began to feel that weekly meetings were too infrequent, especially considering the fact that we often didn't actually meet every week, which was a continuation of our imperfect parenting. Some months, we would meet just twice or perhaps three times.

One of the problems with infrequent meetings was forgetting something that had happened shortly after a previous meeting. I really wanted to use our family meetings to review specific things that our kids had done or not done during the week, both good and bad, so that our discussion of family values could be connected to specific events in their lives. If the kids did something well on a Monday, would Monica or I remember to bring it up at the next meeting? I tried to keep track of these things on a legal pad. Monica utilized the task app on her iPhone. Neither of us was truly successful – things just happened too often and too fast to remember, and we missed a lot of "teachable moments." It was frustrating for both of us, and at times we argued about a methodology to remember everything that arose between meetings. At one point, we even searched for apps to keep us in sync, but we didn't find any that worked for us.

Around the same time, I was sitting on an advisory board for a client's closely held business. The business had significant problems on the shop floor. Delays in production were not being adequately communicated, and this led to a growing number of quality issues and late shipments. I shared this problem with a friend of mine who is a business operations efficiency consultant, hoping to see if he could help. During our discussion, he shared an example about the lean manufacturing process that his business utilized. One of the steps in lean manufacturing is about building processes and then reinforcing them with good, effective communication. He recommends that companies put into place team huddles within each department prior to every shift to improve communication.

This concept caught my attention. The light bulb went off in my head immediately. I don't remember a thing he and I discussed in the remainder of that meeting, because I was too excited to get in the car and call Monica. Unfortunately, being married to a middle-school teacher means she is not very accessible during the day; she can't exactly sit on the phone while 25 sixth-graders get free run of the classroom.

The discussion about "family huddles" may have been the first time I shared one of my "brilliant epiphanies" with Monica, and she actually said, "I think that's a good idea." Her response made me worry that it might *not* be a good idea! We discussed format and decided to try quick 10-minute "huddles" each morning, before Monica headed off to work and before the kids got ready for school. The morning was the best time, as we were all in the same place at the same time. All we had to do was start our day 15 minutes earlier.

For our first family huddle, we used the time to check to see what had gone well and not well the day before, and to review the upcoming day's agenda and responsibilities. It soon became an expectation: family huddles at 6:45 a.m. Of course, this changed based on the bus schedule, but, either way, an expectation was set.

An amazing thing happened. We started to become aware in a very timely manner of what was going on in our children's lives, and it gave us the opportunity to encourage and teach every day. Importantly, it established a free flow of open, honest, and timely communication. It was a reinforcement of daily responsibilities. The kids had to tell us what was going on with them, and what they needed us to do to help them meet those responsibilities. The huddles were of particular benefit to me, because it allowed me to stay in touch with what was going on with them continuously, even on the days when I got home late and the kids were already sleeping. The kids still struggle a little in the mornings to get up and immediately engage in a conversation, but by the time they shake off the grogginess, they are fully engaged.

And whatever happened to our effort to communicate family values? They came up naturally as we dealt with positive and negative things going on in the family. They were becoming the foundation for our discussions and a common language that allowed us to reinforce who we are, what we believe, and how we do things. For example, at one meeting, Elizabeth surprised us with a story about Dominic. One of Dominic's classmates had been spreading rumors about him. Elizabeth reported that Dominic confronted the boy and said, "I know you are making things up about me. I'm not going to let you do that, and I'm not afraid of you." She then turned to Dominic and said, "I'm proud of you for sticking up for yourself."

Hearing this report was heartening on so many levels. As we talked about Dominic's episode, we had an opportunity to discuss the importance of courage and respect for others, and we complemented Elizabeth on her positive attitude about her brother. We talked about integrity and the danger and damage that can be caused by spreading rumors. The discussion made it clear how our family values are expressed and lived in our daily lives – and Dominic no longer asked what family values were. He *knew*. He was living them.

After a while, our family meetings became part of the fabric of family life. The kids would ask when we were holding them, because they had items they wanted to discuss: a trip somewhere, a trampoline for the backyard, and getting paid for their chores. If they wanted something, they had to explain why. Don't get us wrong, we still missed weekend meetings due to busy schedules, but the entire family became motivated to see that the meetings took place. We now had a process within our family for purposeful interaction with our children.

We quickly realized that any conversation with our children presented a teachable moment – an opportunity to talk about values, decisions, and choices. As I look back, our initial practice of reciting our values at the beginning of each family meeting was somewhat effective in reinforcing what they were, but the true benefit came in discussing the application of our values in our daily life. Communicating values is as simple as discussing the "why" behind decisions and the application of "how" in our lives – a practice we will discuss in a later chapter. Over time, family values became a framework for a common language within our family.

The family meetings and huddles are the way that we gather together. In creating this habit, we have become a closer, more cohesive family.

Purpose Not Perfection

All parents aspire to have a family that stays close, communicates, and enjoys spending time together. We want to know what's going on in our children's lives. Additionally, we want to raise children who will make the right choices when we are not there to guide them.

There comes a moment, however, when nearly all of us recognize that we are trapped between the smooth-running household that we aspire to have and the exhausting schedules and commitments that we have. At that moment, we say to ourselves, *There must be a better way.* There must be a way to implement clear channels of communication to assist us in our parenting and the management of our homes.

That "better way" is a culture driven by a formal process to communicate and instill your family's values. The success of any organization, and most importantly the success of a family, is built on the ability to effectively communicate. When you build a series of steps around a desired outcome you ingrain a process that is repeatable. Putting a process in place around communication supports effective interaction. For families, wrapping processes around communication provides the framework to support effective family interaction and the exchange of ideas.

Many people are fooled by today's technology into believing that by synchronizing calendars, texting, and emailing they are increasing their level of communication. Text messages and emails frequently are merely exchanges of information, not ideas. It is the exchange of ideas and the ability to learn from one another that grow our children's experiences and knowledge.

Communicating is a critical skill that will serve your children well in every aspect of their lives. Obviously, gathering for family meals is an important way of learning to communicate. However, the type of communication that takes place during a meal is generally less focused than the type of communication that takes place in a family meeting or huddle.

Instill a culture of communication. The process of family huddles and family meetings will teach your children the importance of sharing and exchanging ideas in a manner that cannot be done through the use of technology alone. Think of huddles and family meetings as focused and structured communication time, free of as many distractions as possible.

We believe it's important that you have a set of meeting rules like, "Everyone's voice is as important as every other voice" and "We don't criticize but support." The meetings are a time to learn from mistakes, and to teach as a cohesive family. Nevertheless, our experience has taught us that effective family meetings and huddles are less about agendas and more about creating an environment for a positive conversation. They don't have to be businesslike. At times, these meetings will be a place for serious discussion, but, in the end, they must be something the children enjoy; they must be positive experiences.

It's important to remember that to effectively interact and exchange ideas, each member of the family (both parents and children) must learn to listen. This is a life skill and tool that parents can teach by being the example, which means not reacting but listening and asking questions so that each child has a chance to learn through their experiences.

There are many ways to practice family meetings or huddles. The best one for you and your family is the one you actually implement and carry out. We have found that the easiest path to happiness in our family is to do something intentionally and consistently.

Gather Together

Define the structure and format of your family meetings or huddles

Write down what the framework of meetings and huddles will look like.

Huddles are more frequent and short (10-15 minutes max).

Meetings are weekly and semi-monthly – a place to expand on conversations and make plans.

Choose the time of day for huddles and how often you will hold them. Be consistent.

Decide on the frequency of family meetings.

Decide on a set of rules to govern the meetings.

Bring your family together

Gather your family and introduce the concept of family huddles and meetings, and why you are going to hold them.

Set the expectation of involvement: "We are a family that communicates."

Discuss why communicating is so important to your family.

Define clearly the times and location of your meetings or huddles.

Be patient

This will take time. Don't get frustrated. Press on and be flexible in what is discussed.

Make your family meetings and huddles interactive, conversational, and fun.

Clarity

Enhance Your Family's

Communication

CHAPTER FOUR

Be The Example

Your actions speak loudly. Your children become what you show them.

Be the example of your values.

Imperfect Parenting

Our family huddles and meetings were definitely leading to better communication within our family, and Monica and I were paying more attention to our own and each other's parenting skills. That focus helped us realize that we had only begun to address all of the ways we needed to communicate. As a result of the family meetings and huddles, we were conversing more frequently and more clearly, and those things are really important. But we had not yet focused on our biggest form of communication: our own behavior.

Monica and I had both read about how most communication is non-verbal, but we really hadn't thought about it in the context of parenting, until we started carefully observing our children. We were a bit startled to realize the extent to which they were walking, talking imitations of us – and all of our imperfections!

I came home one evening to find Monica in the middle of a discussion with Dominic regarding a mess of toys he had been playing with all day.

"This is the fifth time I've asked you to put those toys away," Monica admonished.

Dominic snapped back, "I'm getting to it," but it was obvious he had no intention.

I bellowed my reaction: "Don't you talk to your mother like that. She's your mother. You respect and listen to her."

I turned to Monica, who instead of hugging her chivalrous knight in shining armor, snapped, "Well, where do you think he learned that?"

I was shocked by her response, but I realized that Dominic was mimicking the disrespect I sometimes exhibit when Monica asks me to do something. I felt sick by the realization of what I was teaching my son.

That next night was a cold and snowy Saturday in Northern Ohio. Monica and I were enjoying the peace and quiet of the living room, while the kids were playing in the family room. We started talking about certain behaviors of the children that needed changing and we began to list them.

For me, it was Elizabeth's ignoring me when she was literally five feet in front of me. I would ask her a question, and although she was staring straight at me, she wouldn't respond. After several attempts, I would say, "Elizabeth, did you hear me?"

She would then famously respond, "What? I'm sorry," and proceed to answer the question.

Monica said, "I know," and then, without a pause, started to say, "I'm sorry." As the words came out, I could see the shock on Monica's face, as if she was realizing, *OMG, she's getting that all from me!*

Monica quickly recovered and reminded me of the previous night's event with Dominic.

"You know Dominic's snappy, disrespectful response is not uncommon, and it's not just toward me, but toward his brother and sister as well."

I had no defense to that. It was obvious that he was getting the behavior from me. When someone asks me a question that I consider dumb, it is not uncommon for me to respond with sarcasm. For example, on one occasion, a friend sent us a wrapped gift with a card on top. Monica looked at me and asked what was inside.

I immediately pulled my typical response.

"Really? You see what I see. How the hell do I know?" I was being disrespectful and, if I wanted my son to stop, I needed to stop.

What drove us crazy about Grant was almost too easy. The kid just leaves everything everywhere. On more than one occasion he ran out of socks, and all we had to do was search under couches, corners, play bins, etc. to find all the places he had taken them off and left them. At one point, I was convinced that dyslexia also meant that he had an inability to utilize a coat hanger or even recognize the general location of a closet. As Grant got older, his jacket size and Monica's were about the same. I would grab a coat and start yelling, "Grant, get over here and hang up this coat!" He'd walk into the room, look at me and say, "That's Mom's." I'd throw it in his direction and ask him to hang it up anyway.

As we discussed these bad habits our children had developed, it quickly became obvious that our mantra of "a better me for a better we" was more far-reaching than we had originally thought.

It was then that Monica and I formulated the Example Game. We spent the next couple of weeks keeping a log of every time the kids behaved in a way that reminded us of how one of us acts, so that we could know exactly how bad the problem was. Monica and I soon became experts at identifying each other's bad behavior in our kids – and keeping score. It was eye-opening, to say the least – and, for a while anyway, it was lighthearted and even fun.

I came home one evening and Monica was waiting to pounce.

"How was your day?" I asked tentatively.

"Well," she answered, "I had a nice conversation in the truck with Little Dale tonight. Your mini-me was treating Elizabeth like you treat me at times."

I thought, *Oh boy here we go.* "Which one?"

Monica looked at me with amazement.

"Which one?!" she said. "Dominic, the mini-version of you!"

"What are you talking about, Monica?" I asked. Her coyness could be irritating.

"On the ride home today Elizabeth asked Dominic to help her gather the garbage in the house when we got home, because it's her chore this week. Instead of offering his assistance or simply saying no, he started yelling at her."

"So how is that me?" I asked. Bad question.

Monica replied, "Are you kidding me, Dale? Let's see. He said, 'No, that's your responsibility, stop being lazy and get your job done.' All in a sarcastic and demeaning manner."

I had no rebuttal. It was not uncommon for me to come home from a long day at work and be extremely short and irritable. I was often tired from a full day working with clients, and, more often than not, I brought home a briefcase of unfinished work that I hoped to get to but never did. Exhausted, I would snap at any simple thing that Monica and the kids did, especially when I perceived that they were not taking responsibility for things and, well, being lazy. My behavior was unjustified and needed to change. It was a fair point.

The game continued, and to be honest, it has never stopped. Sometimes, the imitated behavior can be kind of amusing.

One day, we were having guests over for dinner and Elizabeth was in charge of straightening up the kitchen. This was a big task, as it is not unusual to see mail, magazines, homework, and occasionally an unpaid bill left on the kitchen counter. I turned the corner and watched in amazement as Elizabeth opened up a drawer under the counter and swept the entire contents of the counter into the drawer.

"Elizabeth, what you are you doing?" I bellowed.

Elizabeth turned to me and exclaimed, "What? I'm straightening up."

"Sweeping everything into a drawer is not straightening up."

"Sure it is, Dad. That's what Mom does."

Monica had walked into the kitchen during the exchange, so I turned to her – but she had already done a perfect military about-face and was in the midst of fleeing the scene. She knew she'd been caught by her own little mirror.

After our guests left that evening, as Monica and I were cleaning up, I started to tease her about Elizabeth's cleaning methods.

She stopped me and said, "I know, I know, I know."

I continued. "My god, the kids are *becoming* us, complete with our own stupid behavior!"

She laughed. "It's kind of like a horror flick! We are creating the very creatures that are driving us crazy."

Our game could have led to perpetual finger-pointing, but instead we developed a mantra that we both supported: "If we want our children to stop doing it, then we have to go first." From that moment on, we became focused on being good examples and we agreed to remind each other when we were setting a bad example for the kids.

We even brought the kids into the game. One January, Monica was in Florida and the kids and I headed to an indoor community pool to meet up with some friends. I was driving but listening intently to the movie *Sinbad*, which the kids were watching. There are two main characters: Sinbad, who is always positive, and Habib, who always has a negative perspective. After listening for about 20 minutes, I stopped the movie (over the kids' objections) and asked,

"Kids, which of those characters is providing a better example of who you want to be?"

With some reluctance, Dominic yelled, "Sinbad."

"Why?" I asked.

Grant jumped in. "Because he's positive and sees good things in everything."

"And what values does Sinbad share with our values?" I asked.

Elizabeth was ready to join in. "Leadership, positivity, respect, and courage."

"That's right," I said. "What about Habib?"

"He's always negative, always pointing out why they can't instead of why they can," Grant said.

I was so pleased. Here was proof that both good and bad examples come not only from Monica and me, but also from outside the home. We needed to be aware of that to make sure we spoke to it.

As with *Sinbad*, there were plenty of good examples that were as effective in teaching our children as the bad examples. One story I enjoy sharing involved Elizabeth. She was in the backyard with a friend's son, who was five years her junior and who was struggling with his athletic ability at that time. They were playing football and after he dropped the ball for the third time, he looked at Elizabeth and said, "I can't catch it."

"Caden, you can do it," Elizabeth replied. "When life gives you lemons, you make lemonade. Now let's do it again, and I believe you can catch it."

Sure enough, on the next try, he caught the ball. My friend and I just stared at each other in amazement. He said to me, "The apple doesn't fall far from the tree does it?" I just smiled as a proud father and said, "I guess not."

Being an imperfect parent means that we will continue to sprinkle some bad examples in with the good ones. We can't help it.

But if we catch ourselves setting a bad example, Monica and I let the kids know we're wrong and we apologize.

Sometimes, we don't have to catch ourselves because our kids do that for us. Grant takes great pleasure in letting us know when we are not being good examples – not living by our values. He smiles and laughs while he calls us out. At times in our family huddle, I will take the opportunity to address some aspect of our family's life. If there is a smidgen of negativity in my voice, Grant pounces.

"Oh Dad, you are being negative, you are providing a bad example for us. You are not showing positiveness. That's a family value." He smiles ear to ear as he says it. Grant rarely misses an opportunity to remind me when I'm being a bad example, and I love it. It means that he understands and realizes the power of the example.

Let's face it: It is easier to highlight the imperfect examples we provide. But thankfully, we all provide a lot of good examples as well. Our children and yours know what to do, how to act, and the difference between right and wrong because we show them in our actions. They become versions of us because they see us every day, and because they pay attention to what we do, and not only to what we say. Our communication is ongoing. Whether or not we are intentional in our communication, our children are watching and learning and becoming a version of what we show them. In this context, "a better me for a better we" becomes even more important.

Our family improvement project was going pretty well and we were proud of our progress – but, as with so many things, we had no clue what was in store when we peeled back the next layer of the onion.

Purpose Not Perfection

When we speak to our children, we are at least aware that we are communicating and intentionally sending a message. Most of us are much less aware of the powerful and continuous communication going on through our behavior, but social learning theory asserts that most behaviors are learned through observation and modeling. Our children are observing what we do and how we do it. When we talk on the phone, talk to a friend, drive our cars while texting, or interact with a random stranger, they are watching us.

The example we provide is helping to form our children's habits. Our behavior could be the difference between a child who grows up confident and one who does not, or between a child who grows up taking responsibility for his life and one who blames others for his failures. What example are you providing, and are you aware that you are providing it?

We can't expect our children to be what we are not willing to be ourselves. We must be the change we want to see in our children. Part of that change is the realization that we may be wrong about the way we behave and the way we do things. We must live our life the way we want our children to live theirs.

Reflect on how you communicate with your spouse or your parents. Are you showing them the respect you want your children to show you? A parent's behavior toward his or her spouse and others is a strong indicator for their children as to how they should act toward others. We must provide our children a stable foundation of our values that teaches them how to function in society and to be comfortable and confident in it. We must go first.

The example you provide especially influences the culture of communication in your home. If you communicate, so will your children. But if your example is to *not* communicate what's bothering you or to *not* discuss the issues of the house, but instead to keep them bundled up, then your children will learn to do the same. Open, honest, and trust-based communication starts with you. If you find yourself asking, "Why don't the kids get it? We've discussed this many times," remember Albert Einstein's admonishment that "insanity is doing the same thing over and over again and expecting different results." Rather than looking at your children, consider first looking at how the person in the mirror (you) can affect change by changing the example.

The more you think about this, the more you will come to realize that being a good example is a pretty big burden and responsibility – especially when you're an imperfect parent. So what is the solution? First, we need to remind ourselves and our spouses that *we are the example.* I sometimes wish the phrase "Be the Example" were printed on my kids' clothes, so that I would have a constant reminder for myself.

To be the best example, we need to live by our family values. Living by our family values provides a framework that is a continuous reinforcement of who we are, what we believe in, and how we do things.

If we want our children to be honest, we must demonstrate honesty in our behavior. How often have you observed a parent being dishonest about the age of one of his or her children in order to purchase a less expensive movie or amusement park ticket? What message is being sent to your child? Is it really okay? That $10 savings may have been a very expensive lesson about values.

If we want our children to stop or start doing something, then we have to go first. If we want our children to become their best, then we need to become our best self first, and that means being a better parent – a better us. Example is the best teacher. Be the example you want your children to see.

Be The Example

Example: the best teacher

Take notice of what you say and how you do things. Remember to walk the walk and talk the talk that you want your children to see. They are watching.

Jot down some of the things you recently said in front of your children or things you did in front of your children. How do you think your words and actions were interpreted? When you write things down, unforeseen wisdom appears.

Example Game

Watch your kids, observe good and bad habits, and write down where you think they learned each one.

Start working to change the bad habits in both you and your children.

Discuss

It helps to discuss what you have observed and want to improve.

Ask: What are some things I'm doing that I may not be aware of?

Self-police

When you do something that sends a message that is inconsistent with what you want, call yourself out, say I'm sorry, and tell others that it is not the example you want to be.

CHAPTER FIVE

Use A Common Language

Develop a common language to use as a framework for your family's culture of communication.

Imperfect Parenting

As Monica and I became more aware of how the kids modeled our behavior, we naturally started being more careful about the example we were providing. This recognition quickly highlighted a new problem in our parenting: The *language* we were using was not purposeful or consistent. And it was another thing that was causing conflict between Monica and me. This became glaringly obvious one night after an altercation between Elizabeth and Dominic.

I slipped into my old habit and started to lecture the kids. Out came my old stand-by: "Believe in yourself, take responsibility, and take action."

Monica immediately shouted, "Don't you dare start that again!"

The focus had suddenly turned from the kids' bad behavior to mine. *Oh crap,* I thought, *she's right and she caught me.* But it was no longer the somewhat playful "gotcha" we'd throw at each other in the Example Game; this was more serious. I could hear it in Monica's voice.

"Why do you keep going back to that?" she asked.

"They've heard it before," I said, eager to defend myself. "They at least understand the words I'm using."

"Dale, it scares them," Monica said.

"Scares them?" I shot back. I was puzzled. Her description seemed a little extreme.

Monica responded with a sharp tone, like this was a lesson I should have learned a long time ago.

"Yes, Dale, because you are judging them without understanding what is going on and they know it, and that scares them. What good do you think you are doing?"

I realized I had a very narrow window to come up with a logical answer, but at the same time I was reminded of how irritated I had become with Monica. If there was one consistent thing that caused tension between Monica and me, it was the pace at which we approached things.

We are complete opposites. I attack everything with intensity and expect change to be instantaneous. As one of my friends reminds me all the time, "You are a wrestler, you don't know any other way." Monica's approach is definitely more patient, more about "love your children first, second, and third," and everything else later. Not that I disagreed with one, two, or three, but our different approaches caused us years of frustration and tension as a couple and as parents. In my view, she hadn't been doing enough in using our values in her teachings with the children. It was almost as if she didn't care, and it made me feel as though I was the only one paying attention to these big and important ideas.

My irritation was compounded by the fact that this wasn't supposed to be an argument about me, but about what the kids had just done – and it was all unfolding right in front of them. Frustrated, I said, "Well at least I'm doing something to advance the way they think. I haven't heard you do any of it. At least I'm trying."

"Oh, so now since you can't seem to get your whole 'framework of communication' crap correct it's my fault?"

The kids, realizing that they were off the hook and now in the middle of a nasty battlefield, dispersed quickly. I paused for a moment to continue, but Monica was obviously finished with me. As she turned to walk away, she snapped, "You are such an ass."

I was paralyzed. Half of me wanted to chase her down and make sure I won the argument. The other half of me was dazed, wondering what had just happened. We had been talking for months about process and communication and about using the foundation of our values to make sure we captured what we were now calling "teachable moments." Now Monica was telling me it was all "crap"?

I did what I always do when I don't like what's going on in the house. I retreated to my office, sat in my office chair, and stared out the windows at the snow-covered yard. I turned off the lights, except for my desk lamp, and started to reflect. There is something about staring into the dark night that calms me and restores rational thought. I slowly came to the conclusion that I had done exactly what I had been trying to stop. Instead of advancing the way we communicated as a family, I had just taken two steps backward, one with the kids and one with my wife. *Great example of family communication, Dale,* I thought.

It was only Tuesday, but I thought a scotch might help me to relax and think, as I was in no frame of mind to resolve things with Monica and my emotions were running too high. As it turned out, I wouldn't have had the opportunity to resolve anything. Monica had clearly had enough of me and had headed to bed, even though it was only 8:30. Things were not good.

I did the second thing I always do when faced with a tough problem. After staring out the window, I grabbed a yellow legal pad and my blue pen, and started outlining my thoughts.

At the top of the page I wrote "Effective Communication," and underneath it I wrote "Common Language." Monica was right: I'd been preaching for months about the importance of efficient communication in our home in order to improve our family life. As I doodled in the margins with long strokes of my pen, my mind began to free up. We had a framework around communicating – using our values. I stopped doodling and wrote "Values" underneath Common Language. I stared at the words: Effective Communication / Common Language / Values. My doodling continued as I put a big box around all three points. The box brought those three points together – this is how I envisioned it – this was the framework for a common language in our home.

So then why was I frustrated? I did feel that ever since the problems with Grant started, Monica wasn't doing enough, quickly enough. But then I recalled a conversation Monica and I had months earlier in the very room in which I was now sitting, where we had come up with our list of shared values.

We'd spent the time coming up with the values that best reflected our family, with who we were and what we believed in. We had also been doing a good job of discussing what our values mean in our family meetings. So what had gone wrong? I could hear Monica's voice in my head. Through all of this, she had been persistent: "Remember, they are children, you can't forget that." I had forgotten it, because I had forgotten to use our values in the lessons and conversations I'd been having with the kids. Whenever I was tired or under pressure, I resorted to my old lecture. I could see how it would scare the kids: Their dad's default reaction was to instantly judge them.

The truth was that I found it difficult to connect the lessons back to values so the children would understand it. Making the list was easy, but applying the list was tricky. I knew that the kids needed to understand our values before we could expect them to apply them.

We clearly had a common language. Why were we failing in applying them?

As I thought further about the conversations Monica and I had when we made our family values list, I recalled some of her insights.

"Teaching our kids or any kids how those values apply to decisions and actions begins when you make those values real," she'd said. "Just repeating the words and expecting change is unrealistic. If we want our children to live our values and use our values as a common language then we need to make it a conversation."

That's what she meant when she said I wasn't doing any lasting good with my lecture and my snap judgments. I was standing on my soapbox, but no one was listening. In fact, it was quite the opposite. I was shutting down the conversation and turning my audience – my family – away.

And as for my reliance on ideas from business management? She'd said, "You know a lot about business, but not so much about teaching children. When you teach, you have to clearly state your expectations, discuss the complete problem so they see all the perspectives, and let them understand the consequences of their actions and ideas. You have to complete the full 'teaching moment.' You can't just assume they get what you are saying or will draw the same conclusions you do. A teacher doesn't have that luxury; they can't assume. They have to provide everything."

As I thought back to that conversation, I regretted how hard it was to break old habits. As a teacher, Monica spends every day communicating with kids. I needed to give her more credit for her expertise. After all, teachers are trained professionals when it comes to adult/child communication. I clearly wasn't.

I remembered how positive and close Monica and I were that evening when we made our family values list and how we were getting along so well back then. We were in sync, not like tonight, where I was pretty sure that our fourth child, Elvis, the family dog, would be firmly planted in the middle of our bed by the time I got there. Elvis didn't have a lot of responsibilities, but one was clear: "Keep Dad on his side of the bed when I'm mad at him," Monica had always told him. Some nights Monica would jokingly tell him that while I was in the room. Had I remembered and learned the importance of our earlier conversations, I might have enjoyed this evening like we did the night we established our values – and not be sharing my bed with Elvis.

Unfortunately, it would take a couple of days to get back to the discussion. The morning routine left no time for the type of private conversation we needed. Of course, the next two nights I had to work late and, for someone who starts most days at 4:00 a.m., I don't have the emotional wherewithal to be patient and understanding after 8:00 p.m. or so. Elvis enjoyed three solid nights of sleep next to Monica and between us, which I was reminded of each time he stretched all 60 pounds of himself and woke me.

One of the great benefits of the winter is that we normally have a lot less going on on Friday nights, and we use them to relax. I asked Monica for some time to talk, and she willingly agreed, with one condition: "As long as you promise not to be a jerk." I thought I could manage that. She grabbed her standard Friday night glass of "I'm done dealing with 150 children for a couple of days" wine and sat down in the great room. The kids were downstairs enjoying some play time, the fire was going, and the house was peaceful.

"I'm sorry; I didn't handle that correctly the other night."

Monica is not one to quickly say, "Don't worry, it's okay," and she patiently waited to hear more. I continued.

"I know that everything we are doing is not 'natural' and it takes time. I see the benefits of our efforts, and I appreciate that patience is not one of my best attributes."

I revisited our discussion about using our values to provide what we've been calling teachable moments to the kids. I promised to once again bury the old "take responsibility, take action" lecture and to foster conversation instead. And I assured her that I understood the need to discuss with the kids all the facets of each teachable moment: our expectations, their understanding the problem, the need to see all the perspectives, and the consequences associated with their actions.

Monica had been sitting on our couch with her feet tucked under her and almost no expression on her face. Like a good poker player, she was finally ready to show her cards.

"You know, I get it, you care about the family and kids. I get it. It's one of the reasons I really love you. You are passionate and when you go after something, especially when it's about family, you go after it. But...."

I remember thinking how much I hate the word "but." All the stuff that we don't want to hear comes right after "but."

Monica continued. "But you have to remember that you're not here a lot of the time. I *do* use our values in my discussions with the kids and use them to provide guidance and teach. I may not do it as relentlessly as you do, and, to be honest, you still need to remember that they are kids. You always tell me when it comes to financial things, 'Trust me, I know what I'm talking about, this is what I do for a living.' Well, guess what? Teaching children is what *I* do for a living, so you should take some pointers from me about how to communicate with the kids. Nothing happens quickly, it's about consistency and clarity of your message. We will get there. You just have to be patient."

I was shocked. It was as though she spent three days perfectly formulating her response to me. She had even framed what I had been trying to figure out: the idea of a common, clear, and consistent language. There was nothing I could say. I just looked at her and said, "Dear, you're absolutely right."

There was no hesitation on her part. "I know," she said, "That's how moms roll."

It was obvious by the smirk on her face that she enjoyed being able to make that comment. She'd earned it.

Over time, I began to appreciate that Monica was, in fact, embracing the process and communication systems we had put in place. She frequently used our family values as a way to begin an intentional conversation with our kids, using a common language to clarify what we wanted. I had to admit that her patience was paying off. It was evident in a conversation she had one day with Elizabeth.

Elizabeth came home from school and wanted to talk to Monica. She was upset because a boy and girl in her classroom kept kissing when their teacher turned her back to the class. Elizabeth and her classmates were still in elementary school, but at an age when boys and girls are first starting to notice each other. Monica and Elizabeth discussed Elizabeth's feelings, and Monica subtly pointed out that perhaps the reason that Elizabeth was upset was that her classmates' behavior was not in line with Elizabeth's values (our family's values) regarding integrity, leadership, and respect, and so she was therefore aware that it was not appropriate behavior. This explanation helped calm Elizabeth and gave her a framework (foundation) for understanding her feelings.

When Monica shared this story with me, she explained what she had done.

"Plugging into an experience that Elizabeth brought home from school was a really effective way of talking about values," Monica said, "because she was not the subject of the discussion. It was not about what she did or didn't do, and it worked really well. It was a great example of how we can learn from others' actions, right or wrong."

I was glad to hear stories like this and Monica never hesitated to share them – partially, I'm convinced, as her way of saying, "See, I know what I'm doing. So stop telling me I'm not doing enough." I got the message – finally.

Learning to communicate with the kids in a common language around our family values was going to take time and patience, and we would each adopt these new habits in our own way with our own style, and it was going to take time to bring positive change to our family.

We took moments of validation when we could get them. At times, raising children can be a continuous struggle, because there is rarely an immediate indication that your efforts are effective. It was no different in our attempt to develop a culture of communication and a common language in our family. Monica and I were being more intentional, our conversations with the kids were more fluent, and our arguments with each other over our parenting styles became much less intense, but we still wondered whether we were making an impact.

Then, one day, we received some affirmation, as we watched Elizabeth reprimand Elvis. It seemed that Elvis had done something of which Elizabeth didn't approve, and she had him sitting, chin up, looking her right in the eye.

"Elvis, you can't do that. You need to treat people how you want to be treated. That's a family value: respect. Okay? Remember, I love you."

She then gave him a big hug. I watched as his tail started wagging excitedly. If I had a tail, it would have been wagging excitedly too. She was listening, she was learning, and she was living our values. I was proud of her. A culture of communication was being formed, with love and trust as the cornerstone. Small moments like watching Elizabeth and Elvis encouraged us to press on.

Purpose Not Perfection

Sociologists tell us that common language is a critical component of every culture, not only because it facilitates communication, but also because it strengthens a sense of identity or belonging among members of the culture. The shared values reaffirm the individual's sense of belonging, provide comfort, and build trust.

The cornerstone of your family's common language is your values. Your family's values give you a framework or starting point for talking with your children about problems, resolving disputes, correcting misbehavior, and rewarding positive actions. Not only does this framework help you direct your communication, but it also provides your children with familiar words and direction. It gives them clarity and you the comfort that the teachable moment was understood in the way you intended. It makes the conversation easier because you know where to start: with your values.

As those values become part of your regular vocabulary, they communicate far more than the simple meaning of the word because they carry with them past discussions and shared experiences that enhance the meaning. A consistent discussion of values tells your children that the values are important to you and should be important to them too. Over time, you will find that your children will use your family's common language when communicating with you or their siblings. Trust is formed around communication and allows open and honest dialogue.

The most important common language in any home should be the continuous reminder to your children that you love them. "I love you" should be your first and foremost common language. With love, you build trust, and with love and trust, anything is possible.

A common language is not an afterthought to your efforts to become a better family. It's the glue that cements you together.

Use A Common Language

Remember: "I love you"

"I love you" is the foundation of your family's common language.

Your culture of communication

When an event occurs and you need to respond, start with a family value to give direction to the conversation.

Using your values in teachable moments reminds your children that your family's values are important.

CHAPTER SIX

Respond, Don't React

Choose to respond and control your emotions by starting with a pause.

Imperfect Parenting

As mentioned with my infamous "take responsibility, take action" lecture, I have a bad habit of repeating sage advice over and over and over again. Another one of my favorites is "Reduce chaos to increase happiness." You may wonder if that advice is even possible in a house full of busy children and busy parents, but I have observed that many of the problems we face as parents are self-inflicted. The largest number of arguments among Monica and the kids, Monica and me, and the kids and me, are about chaos, or a lack of organization.

As someone with attention deficit hyperactivity disorder (ADHD), I've learned one thing: If I don't keep myself organized and keep lists, my personal life becomes completely reactionary and doesn't leave room for a great deal of success and happiness. I've tried to impress upon my family the benefits of organization. Let's just say I'm not yet ready to mark this down as one of my highly successful accomplishments. And, if I'm being honest, it's the lack of organization of the rest of my family that sets me off and most frequently leads to what I refer to as my *Oh crap, I'm doing it again* moments.

The following is not an uncommon story in our home. I was mentally and emotionally trying to wind down after work, and the only step I'd taken was to unbutton the top button of my shirt and loosen my tie ever so slightly. Before she even said hello, Monica pounced.

"You need to talk to your son." The words "your son" immediately annoyed me. Those words – not "our son" but "your son" – instantly told me she was not happy with one of the boys.

My response or reaction to things is usually driven by the time of day. In the mornings, I'm usually up an hour or so before anyone else and at my best mentally and emotionally. I am much better about pausing and thinking about how I can add value to a situation. By evening, I've pretty much exhausted my capacity to pause and be thoughtful.

As I thought about "my son," I walked to the refrigerator to take out my dinner. All the servings were neatly organized on one plate and covered with Saran wrap – a kindness for which I was always grateful. When I made eye contact with Monica, she continued.

"Grant wasn't prepared for school this morning, and when I addressed it with him he yelled at me and treated me disrespectfully."

I knew what she wanted: for me to resolve the situation and have a conversation with Grant around respect. *But why the heck do I need to get involved?* I kept that thought to myself – sort of – and calmly asked Monica, "So how did your conversation about respect go with him?"

Monica looked at me with clear displeasure and responded,

"We didn't have a conversation. He was going to be late for school. So after yelling at him, I stopped so he could get what he needed done and get on the bus."

"So let me get this straight," I said, without pausing and with a sharp tone, "you know the conversation you need to have with him, you two have been home for several hours, you've had some time to relax from your day, and now you want me, who just got home – you want me to go address this?"

Monica's one word response ignited the next 45 minutes of chaos in our house: "YEP."

I slammed my dinner plate down and headed off to find Grant. In that short walk to Grant's room, my anger grew. I was fuming – mad at Monica for making me deal with this – and it was all about to become Grant's misfortune. As I hit the threshold of Grant's bedroom door, I recalled my father's lectures that "you never, never, never disrespect your mother, ever" and his 44-inch belt that would be delivered to my backside for doing so.

So, without pause, full of emotion, I said, "Why did you disrespect your mother this morning?"

Grant, obviously caught off guard by my sudden presence, was searching for a response when I decided I was not going to wait for a reply.

"How many times have I told you that you do not talk back to your mother or any other adult? Furthermore, respect is one of our family values, and I expect you to live up to that value."

Grant, with a look of utter befuddlement, meekly asked, "What did I do?"

Oh crap, I thought, *I'm doing it again.* I paused to breathe and collect my thoughts.

With my emotions in check I said him, "Okay, Grant. Your mother said because you were disorganized and ill-prepared for school today, the two of you had an argument and she felt that you were disrespectful in how you reacted."

Grant immediately started defending himself.

"Dad, I asked Mom to get me a poster board for my project and she didn't. She said she would."

Struggling to not react to Grant's defensiveness, I replied, "Okay. First, calm down." I could just as easily have said, *Don't act like I acted before.* What a terrible example I had been!

I then continued. "What is the poster board for?"

"My book report project," Grand replied.

Through the remainder of our conversation, I picked up some confusion between Monica and Grant about what had been communicated. Did they agree about who owned the responsibility of getting the poster board? Grant assumed that since he told his mother, he had released his responsibility, a common practice among kids. At least, among *our* kids.

Monica, whose first thought is always to take care of her children, has a habit of saying yes to their requests, even though she might be in the middle of something else. She inevitably forgets and the request goes unfulfilled. This is what always happens when communication is not clear: chaos ensues. I finished my conversation with Grant by reminding him that it was his project and therefore his responsibility to get the needed supplies.

"Grant," I said, "the responsibility remains yours from beginning to end. You never release the responsibility."

I explained to him that he had to check in and remind those who made promises to help him, and I reminded him that it was not fair to ask his mother for things when she was in the middle of dealing with several other matters.

I headed to the family room, where Monica was grading papers. Before I could get seated Monica said, "Well, did you talk to him?"

"Yep." I replied.

It was obvious Monica didn't deem that to be enough information.

"And?" she asked.

I tried to calmly bring up a recurring theme in our house regarding communication, responsibility, and organization, but needless to say I could have done a better job.

"Well, it appears there was some miscommunication around him thinking you were going to get a poster board, when it was needed, him taking responsibility to make sure that you were getting it in a timely manner, and, well, I'm guessing just an overall lack communication and organization that caused the problem."

The phrase "lack of communication and organization" is one that sets off my lovely bride.

Monica, now defending herself and visibly upset said, "Oh, this is now my fault? He did not remind me he needed it, and he should know not to ask for anything when I'm in the middle of doing something else."

I foolishly decided to take a step onto my soapbox.

"Monica, I don't know why you are surprised. How many times have I told you, when the kids ask you to do something or get something while you are in the middle of something else, you have to tell them, 'No, bring this up later in a family huddle or meeting'? You can't say, 'Okay,' which implies that you have taken ownership and responsibility. No one asks about it later, and *boom*, we are stuck right back where you two were this morning, arguing about a lack of organization and communication. Then, I come home after a full day and I have to fix a problem that was avoidable, if you would just get organized and communicate."

I couldn't resist the urge to get in one last dig.

"Besides, it's your example that is the very reason Grant continues to be as disorganized as he is."

Monica was doing what she always does during my soapbox lectures. Nothing – just a blank stare, no emotion, hiding her obvious frustration with me. I paused momentarily for a response but, instead of waiting patiently, I said to her, "Well?"

Monica looked at me, slowly got up from the couch, said, "You're an ass," and headed off to bed.

Hello, Elvis!

Now there is good news and bad news in these types of situations in our home. First, they still happen. I'm sorry if you were hoping to hear "and now we don't even argue at all!"

We were and continue to be imperfect parents and imperfect spouses. However, years ago this type of argument would have caused a whole week of silent treatment between the two of us. The only communication we would have given each other during that time were one word answers to questions like, "Can you pick up Grant tonight from Boy Scouts at 8:30 p.m.?" I would reply "yes," and that would be the end of it.

The good news is that today we are quicker to resolve our disagreements. The morning after my soapbox lecture, after Monica finished her shower, I came up from my home office, stood in front of her as she stood in her pink robe, put my hands on each of her arms, and confessed.

"Dear, I had another 'Oh crap, I did it again' moment. I didn't respond. I reacted."

She continued the blank stare from the night before.

"I'm sorry," I said. "I need to keep working on responding and not reacting."

Her reply was a simple: "I know." She didn't say that it was okay, but we both understood each other. We both have our imperfections and reacting is one of mine. We are getting better – we'll never be perfect, but we are getting better.

At some point, identifying "respond versus react" moments became another game that Monica and I would play, but it was one that I would continuously lose. Every now and then, I'd catch Monica heading off to react to something the kids had done, but I was by far the worse offender. Over time, we realized that when we reacted rather than responded, we'd regret the lost opportunity for a teachable moment. It seemed like it happened daily in our house.

To be honest, there are times when Monica or I have called each other out, but at those moments there is simply too much emotion in the room to stop and respond. Sometimes the emotion of the moment simply overcomes all rational thought.

At one point, we saw that the kids were reacting to everything and not responding. We weren't concerned about them providing a teachable moment to each other. Instead, we simply hoped they would engage in a conversation rather than a yelling match. So, for several weeks, we gave everyone in the house permission to stop another family member that was reacting and say, "Are you responding or reacting?" We agreed that, when that happened, the person that was called out had to stop, breathe, think, and respond.

As with the Example Game, Grant was the master of the Respond versus React game. Grant is the most disorganized of the three kids, and there was ample opportunity to react to him, because something almost always seemed lost. He used the Respond versus React game to his full advantage and would stop me in my tracks with, "Dad, are you responding or reacting?"

Grant always stopped me with a grin on his face, because he knew exactly what he was doing. I enjoyed him catching me, because it quickly changed my mood and made me smile. Over time, I've gotten better at getting to the teachable moment without being distracted by that grin of his.

We sometimes still react rather than respond, but we are much more aware of our communication. Sometimes we catch ourselves mid-stream (*Oh crap, I'm doing it again...*) and change direction with an apology to the child and a positive conversation rather than a lecture. I know Monica and I will never get to the point where we always respond versus react, but that's just part of being an imperfect parent.

Purpose Not Perfection

A reaction is an immediate, emotional response to an event that has just occurred. There is no time to gather one's thoughts or to bring emotions under control. Consequently, many times the reaction is irrational, disproportionate, and ineffective as a teachable moment.

The loss of a teachable moment is only one of many reasons that we should strive to respond to our children rather than to react. Because a reaction is typically quick and strongly emotional, it is usually perceived as aggressive and threatening. The normal response to such a threat is fear and anger, neither of which improves the relationship or communication between a parent and a child. In fact, a pattern of emotional reactions to problems can destroy a family's culture of communication. It makes it far less likely that our children will trust that they can bring their problems to us and seek our help without exposing themselves to the pain of our anger.

Additionally, if we regularly react rather than respond to difficult situations, our example is teaching our children to do the same thing. (Remember, the awesome power of example.) To respond requires that we pause and take a moment to formulate a less emotional and more rational response to the situation. By taking time to gather our thoughts, we allow ourselves to be more directed in the way we address a particular situation. What typically follows is a conversation rather than a shouting match. A reasoned response invites a similar response from our children and increases the likelihood that our message will be heard and understood.

As imperfect parents, there will be times when we react rather than respond, and that is understandable. Reacting is a very natural human response, almost a primal response. Think about animals in nature: a deer in the woods that hears a sound it did not expect. Its primal response is not to pause and be thoughtful about what it heard, but to react and run. In the same way, we are perhaps hardwired to react to strong emotional situations with a similar strong response. Responding requires that we fight the urge to react and instead process information and communicate thoughtfully.

Even when we react rather than respond to our children, there is a way to turn those occasions into teachable moments. It starts by catching oneself and then saying, "I'm sorry for reacting that way." The words "I'm sorry" are, unfortunately, not said enough by parents or between spouses. "I'm sorry" is an admission that you are not perfect but that you are willing to try. Those simple words create an opportunity to replace our emotionally filled reaction with a rational response.

When we tell our spouse "I'm sorry" in front of our children, we teach a valuable lesson about respect. Monica and I have learned that when we use those two words, we send a positive message to our children and, at the same time, improve our relationship. When we tell our children "I'm sorry" for reacting rather than responding, we are reinforcing the importance of a thoughtful response and are building trust. We are also teaching them how to move from a reaction to a response.

Responding creates a positive culture of communication within the family, a culture built on trust. A culture of communication assures that our actions educate our children. Choose to respond rather than to react. It's easier said than done, but it is possible. Over time, you'll find that responding rather than reacting becomes a habit. When you fail to respond, remember that a pause and an "I'm sorry" are helpful tools for getting back on track. It is an acknowledgment that you are not perfect but care enough to try.

Respond, Don't React

Pause

Stop, gather your thoughts, remove the emotion, and respond – optimize the teachable moment.

Fight the urge to react. Bite your tongue if need be.

Be intentional in the way you respond. This is an opportunity to teach.

Common language

Don't forget your family's common language: your values. It will give you guidance when you respond.

I'm sorry

Reacting is inevitable. As a matter of fact, it is human nature. So when it does happen, say "I'm sorry" and respond the way you should have.

You are the example

The way you respond or react is providing the example you will see in your children.

CHAPTER SEVEN

Get Off The Soapbox

Step down from your soapbox and into a conversation where listening builds trust.

Imperfect Parenting

I started to feel that I was making great progress communicating with our kids, and there were some undeniable improvements in our family's life. There were more moments where I felt like I was getting the parenting thing totally under control. I was certainly making progress in pausing before responding to my children in order to capitalize on those teachable moments. But sometimes what appears to be progress is more akin to running on a treadmill. It soon became clear that my problem wasn't the pause; it was the response.

As much as I fight it, I am a soapbox guy. After that pause, I have an insatiable desire to, in that one teachable moment, transfer to my children all of what is in my head and all of the wisdom of my experiences. If I see something that needs correcting, I eagerly launch into a college-level lecture. This isn't an occasional thing. The opportunities for providing this kind of guidance are everywhere. Over time, I came to realize that the lectures were a big reason why my kids didn't trust me the way they trusted Monica.

One spring evening, I was relaxing with a cup of coffee, attempting to improve my golf game by reading *Golf Digest* and contemplating whether a new driver really would "change my game." The peace was interrupted when Elizabeth, who was entertaining a friend, shrieked, "Dad! Dominic is annoying us!"

I calmly asked Dominic to join me in the kitchen. So far so good – I didn't react. When he joined me, I would respond. But when someone disturbs the peace, particularly *my* peace, the result is unlikely to be a conversation. It's prime time for a soapbox lecture. Before Dominic was halfway to the kitchen, I had already decided that the day's lecture was going to be on responsibility and appreciating how one's decisions affect others. In this case, honoring the value of respect required that he decide to leave his sister and her friend alone and not pester them.

I began my lecture.

"Dominic, I know you are aware of our family value, respect. What's missing here is you taking the responsibility to live it."

At that moment it may have made sense to pause and ask him a question. But I was firmly on my soapbox and had no intention of stepping down. I didn't stop with just the one point about respect. Instead, I continued with a dissertation on the importance of taking his sister's perspective – understanding the message people are sending you and changing your behavior appropriately. Now that I was on a roll, I moved onto a brief lecture concerning Dominic's decision-making process, a process so defective that it permitted him to conclude that it was okay to irritate his sister.

I asked rhetorically, "So how do you decide it is okay to pester your sister and her friend?"

I'm sure I could have continued for another 30 minutes, but Monica was in the family room reading and had reached her level of intolerance for my lecture.

"Dale," she yelled. "Stop the lecture."

If it had been 12 months earlier, there was no way I would have stopped. I would have kept going and likely, at some point, snapped and gotten on a soapbox with Monica too. But we were changing. We were becoming aware of ourselves, our actions, and, most importantly, the example we were giving our kids. So I stopped and told Dominic to leave his sister alone and find something else to do.

Later that evening, after Monica was finished reading and I had decided against the shiny new golf club, I teased her about stifling my opportunity to share my wisdom with Dominic.

Monica must have been in the mood to share, because without pause she said, "I paid extra attention this week to things that might cause me to get on my soapbox with our kids and my students, and I found it somewhat enlightening. When I didn't lecture, but instead had a conversation, I gained their trust. When I listened and tried to take their perspective, they actually were willing to share more."

Monica must have seen the puzzled look on my face, which screamed, *What the hell are you talking about?*

"You know, Dale," she said, "not everything our kids do wrong needs to be a long discussion. If you say something short, simple, and direct, sometimes it's all you need."

We had been circling around this idea for months – the idea that my lectures scared the kids and prevented them from trusting me. And finally, what she was saying seemed to be making sense.

She continued. "Take, for instance, when Grant was being ridiculed at school for the struggles he has at reading aloud in the classroom. Like any mother, I consoled him. But I also asked him how he felt and used the time to talk things out. We discussed my experiences where someone had said things to me that were hurtful or could've been upsetting, and I explained how we often have to turn the other cheek and ignore those hurtful incidents. I could only do that because it was so clear that he was ready to listen."

I thought I saw a hole in her argument.

"That's fine for those moments when someone is suffering and you are discussing your understanding of their perspective, but how would that work when one of the kids is causing the issue like Dominic was this evening? I could go to my grave waiting for him to feel like listening."

"Sometimes, I just ask questions," Monica responded. "I'll bet if you had asked Dominic some questions about his motivations tonight, he would've figured out he was wrong without a lecture."

I hate when I push Monica into proving I'm wrong, but she was right. The issue was that I didn't give the children a chance to talk. I'm impatient, and I want to see the learning process move quickly. In my professional world, I do the opposite. I ask questions all the time – the client talking more, me listening more. I try to figure out how they are thinking about a particular problem – not what they did, but what knowledge or experience they used to arrive at that point in the thought process. When I do that, I learn how they think, I gain their trust, and I can help them solve problems by changing the way they think about a particular issue. But with the kids, I just jump on the soapbox – the exact opposite of what I do with my clients.

I got the message, but I didn't take it to heart until a few months later.

It was a summer night, warm and calm, and eight families had gathered at the neighborhood party house. It had a swing set, a trampoline, a zip line, and tree houses to keep the kids busy while the parents relaxed. It was dark out, just past 9:00 p.m. The kids were playing, and I was enjoying a conversation with my friend Nick about a particular business he was considering buying.

Out of the nowhere, my neighbor showed up with Grant, holding the back of his shirt. My neighbor was infuriated.

"Do you know what your son just did?"

I didn't have a moment to open my mouth before he continued.

"He just called my daughter a lesbian. He called her that and in front of her friends. Name calling is unacceptable and not welcome in my home. You need to deal with this."

It was one of those moments that is completely disorienting. You have to respond, but you don't have time to absorb and contemplate the speed of the information you're receiving.

"I got it," I said as my neighbor walked away. Fuming, I looked at Grant and said, "Go home now. You've embarrassed yourself and the family."

As Grant headed off crying, I excused myself from the conversation I was having and started home, hot on Grant's trail. You would have thought that the five-minute walk would have calmed me down, but I was only getting angrier over being embarrassed in front of my buddies and neighbors. Would they think that I was raising a bunch of bigoted kids? Bullies?

Monica was already in bed; she had not been feeling well that evening and had turned in early. I was going to have to deal with Grant myself. By the time I came barging into the house, Grant had made it to his bedroom.

I rushed toward him and started yelling, "What were you thinking? Why would you call someone that? You've embarrassed yourself and our family!"

I did not ask any questions, I did not listen, and there was no discussion about respect or any other reference to our family values.

Two minutes into my angry lecture, Grant, who was 12 years old at the time, was cowering at the top of his bed, wrapped up into a ball, hugging his pillow, with tears gushing. He softly cried, "I don't know why."

His response only infuriated me more – *He didn't understand his own actions?* – and I amped up my lecture and verbal assault.

"Why would you call someone that?"

At that moment, something told me to pause – maybe it was Grant's crying or simply that moment of exhaustion that follows when you have completely vented your anger.

I stopped, I took a breath, and I calmly asked Grant, "Do you even know what a lesbian is?"

His answer stopped me dead in my tracks.

"No, I don't know what that means," Grant said.

I was stunned and at a complete loss for words.

I calmed down, I paused again, and then I hopped on my soapbox.

"Grant, why would you even use a word that you don't understand?" I went on and on, and his tears didn't stop even though I was no longer yelling.

As I began to run out of steam, the embarrassment of the incident faded and I started to notice Grant, still balled up and crying. My lecture had completely ignored his pain, and I was washed over with guilt. I remembered my conversation with Monica about lectures versus conversations. I realized how wrong my lecture had been. I feared I had done irreparable damage to my relationship with Grant.

I walked out of his room to collect myself. I grabbed the railing that overlooked our two-story great room with both hands, leaned into it, and hung my head. *What the heck am I doing?* Even though I had calmed down, I was lecturing. I realized that I needed to put myself in his shoes, from the moment the event occurred to now. After all that had transpired, he still didn't know what the word he used meant. He was in trouble, and in pain, and he didn't even know why.

My goal as a father is to help my son grow into a young man and provide guidance and experience to shape how his decision-making process evolves. I know all these things are critical to how he arrives at good and positive life choices. I feared that all I had done over the last several minutes was to destroy any remaining trust he had in our relationship.

What if he comes across a very difficult or deep crisis moment in his life? Why would he come to me, if he believed all he would get was a lecture? I knew that wouldn't actually be true, but, up to this point, he had no reason to believe otherwise. At that moment, I prayed to God to save me from my stupid self.

I walked back into Grant's room. He hadn't budged from his spot in the bed, still curled up and still sobbing. I sat next to him, put my arm around him, and started with an apology.

"Grant, I'm sorry. I overreacted. Can we have a conversation about this?"

Grant was still not ready to talk, but he nodded his head up and down, while he grasped his blanket tightly. I knew at that point that the less I talked and the more I listened the better chance I had at rebuilding trust. I asked him if he wanted to know the meaning of the word he used, and he again nodded affirmatively. I explained the meaning and that it was insensitive to use it in the way he did. I talked about how calling people names under any circumstances was, as my friend had said, unacceptable.

He finally spoke. "Dad, I never meant to hurt anyone. I had no idea that's what it meant."

My response was slow and soft. "I know, Grant. You would never hurt anyone intentionally."

Grant continued. "Dad, I feel really bad. I need to apologize to Jen. I hope she is okay."

The one thing I always admired about Grant was his compassion for others. You could find him entertaining a 4-year-old at a party and 30 minutes later see him sitting with a grandparent, having a pleasant conversation.

Grant and I spoke for another 30 minutes or so. I guided our conversation around the things we hear, learn, and experience and how they provide us knowledge to use as we grow as individuals. Grant did a lot of the talking, and repeated his desire to go to our neighbors the next day to apologize.

The next day, my neighbor, his daughter, Grant, and I met at their home. Grant apologized, as did my neighbor for the way he reacted. Grant learned a valuable lesson that day – well, he learned several – but one was the courage it takes to apologize for your wrongs, face them, and not run from them. It was an experience I'm positive he'll remember forever.

What I learned that day was another life-changing moment. I knew that the kids always had a lot more trust in Monica than me. I assumed that it was because she was around more than me, and she always provided the comfort they needed. I was the disciplinarian, the relentless lecturer about learning and growing. Now I realized that it was more than that. The kids trusted Monica because they felt safe when talking to her.

I vividly recall the fear I had that evening as I stood over the railing, worrying that I had destroyed Grant's trust in my ability to protect him, to be reasonable, to understand, to talk about a difficult situation without blowing up. He might love me, but without trust, he would never come to me for guidance, direction, safety, or comfort. This lesson ate at me for months, and I've worked to fix my relationship with Grant. I now appreciate that maintaining a trusting relationship with my children is a never-ending journey, and that trust can be easily damaged.

I also learned that taking a moment to pause and respond is not enough. The true lessons come when we learn to build relationships through conversations, taking time to understand our child's perspective, and helping our child develop his or her decision-making process. It's all built on trust, and that is a journey, not a destination.

I'm happy to report that I have restored my relationship with Grant, and I've improved the trust between all of my kids and me, by lecturing less and conversing more. The kids used to always go to Monica first, assuming that she would come to me on their behalf. That is no longer the case. As I have reduced the number of lectures and increased the conversations, the kids do come talk to me without her. That tells me I'm in the process of righting my wrongs.

I teach my children that there is something to be learned from everything, good and bad. I'm grateful for the lesson I learned from my blow-up with Grant. It's one that caused me such pain that it is etched in my brain as a very strong reminder of how crucial trust is and how important conversations are in building trust and creating a culture of communication.

Our entire family has learned and gotten used to the art of conversation. Monica and I have observed that if we take time to understand our children's perspective, we gain a better understanding of their thought processes. It is often easier and more effective to help our kids change their thought process than it is to change a specific decision or behavior. Occasionally, it does make sense to get on the soapbox, such as Monica's lecture to me about the need to avoid lectures. But, more often than not, a good conversation is more effective.

Purpose Not Perfection

The problem with the soapbox is that when we engage in one-way communication, we lose an opportunity to build trust in our relationship with our child. It has been said that trust is simply "the unquestioned belief that the other person has your best interest at heart." That sounds a lot like a definition of love, but love and trust are not quite the same thing. Our children may know we love them, but still not trust that they can come to us with every problem. Trust gives our children the comfort of knowing that they can seek our advice or share difficulties in their lives without any fear of losing our love. You can't, after all, help children deal with problems that you don't know exist. A culture of communication will build trust, and trust gives you a chance.

The first step in getting off the soapbox is to know when you are on it. When talking with your children, ask yourself the following question: *Am I talking at them or with them?* If there is not a positive exchange of ideas between you and your child, it is quite likely that you are giving an ineffective lecture and missing an opportunity to teach. If you are ordering your child to listen, it's a good sign that you are not listening to yourself.

It is a good exercise to think about the last time you received a lecture. Do you remember what was said? Did you walk away inspired and thankful for the person taking the time to teach you and provide you feedback? Did you say to yourself, *They really like and care about me?* Or did you say, *They didn't listen to a word I said or even attempt to understand my perspective?* Did the lecture leave you thinking about the matter being discussed or simply angry at being treated the way you were? It's reasonable to assume that our children react the same way when we lecture them.

We need to listen to our kids, and part of being a good listener is to be empathetic. In this context, empathy is simply putting yourself in your child's place to better understand how they are thinking and what they are feeling. When we acknowledge our child's feelings, we create an environment that is conducive to an open exchange. Our kids will come to us knowing that they won't get a lecture, but a conversation.

The techniques described above are forms of "active listening." They are important tools to use with our children, because nonjudgmental conversation builds trust and respect and teaches our children that it is safe to share things with us. It opens our children up to having the difficult conversations that inevitably take place between a parent and child.

Get Off The Soapbox

Trust

Trust and love become the foundation for good communication.

When you communicate and engage in understanding the other person's perspective, you build trust.

When your child knows that you will listen and not lecture, it is more likely they will come to you for guidance and help when they are struggling with something.

Talk "with" not "at"

Have conversations, not lectures. You'll know the difference.

Remember how you react emotionally when you are lectured. There is no listening or learning. The same goes for your kids. A conversation allows both of you to learn.

Focus

Don't multitask. Instead, give your children your full attention. It sends a message to them about how important they are. It also provides the example of how they should treat others.

Active listening

Listen first, speak second.

Be sure you understand their perspective before you respond.

Be empathetic, understand their perspective.

CHAPTER EIGHT

Give Them The 'Why'

The learning and experience is in the why. Give them the why.

Imperfect Parenting

Getting off the soapbox and engaging in conversation was a big change for me, but also one that I thoroughly enjoyed. No matter how well you think you know your kids, you will know them better the more you talk with them. Of course, everything comes with a price, and the price of more conversations is the requirement to answer more questions. As every parent knows, there is no more frequent or important question than "Why?"

There are times that this question can set us off like a firecracker. This happened one evening, as I was comfortably perched at my desk working. I heard Monica's voice come screeching from downstairs: "Because I said so!"

Sensing the tension and frustration in Monica's voice, I got up to help.

"What's going on?" I asked.

She quickly answered. "I've been asking your children all week to pick up the toys and garden tools from the backyard before it starts snowing and they haven't done it yet."

My children. This was a bad sign. I shook my head, acknowledging her frustration.

"And what caused the 'because I said so' reaction?" I asked.

"I'm tired of them asking 'why' every time I ask them to do something!"

While I had some thoughts to share regarding her how she handled the situation, I figured I'd be better off leaving the scene of the crime and addressing the issue with "my children" if I wanted to stay in Monica's good graces the rest of the day.

I headed upstairs and gathered the three kids.

"Okay guys, it's obvious that your mother has asked you several times to pick up the backyard before it starts snowing, so why do you think she wants that done?"

Dominic, who appeared to be playing both sides of the game, immediately offered: "Because she said so."

With a smile I said, "I get that, but why?"

Grant jumped in. "Because it's our mess and our responsibility."

I was encouraged by this early insight.

"Exactly. It's your stuff, you brought it out, you played with it, and it is your responsibility to put it away. Thanks, Grant. Great answer. But why else?"

All I got in response were three shoulder shrugs and complete silence.

"It's now November. The weather is getting colder. What may happen?"

Elizabeth, as if playing Jeopardy, yelled, "Snow! I like snow! It means we can sled."

You can't blame her for the enthusiasm for winter activities. We have two sledding hills in our backyard and one drops directly into a big sand pit.

"Correct," I replied. "What happens to our stuff when the snow hits?"

Grant returned to the conversation. "It all gets buried for the winter."

"Again, nice job. And then what? Then what happens?" Again, three shoulder shrugs. I answered my own question: "It gets ruined from the wet and cold and we have to throw it out and buy new stuff."

I was tempted to continue with the "money doesn't grow on trees" lecture, but I felt like I had made my point, so I attempted a conclusion.

"First, it's your responsibility, and second, we don't want the toys and tools that are not put away to get ruined. So what should we do?"

All three answered simultaneously but without a lot of excitement, "Go pick them up."

"Great. Whether you are excited about it or not, it needs to be finished. One final thought: Some of that stuff won't be used until the spring, so put that stuff in the basement." With that, they dispersed to clean up the yard.

I figured I was on a roll, so I went downstairs to see if I could transform my now perfect parenting into perfect husbanding.

Monica looked at me as I entered the room. "Did you threaten them?"

I was a little insulted that she felt that was the only tool in my bag, but I simply said, "Nope, just gave them the why."

She looked at me inquisitively. "What?"

"I thought it would be more helpful long-term for them to understand why you've been asking them to pick up their things," I said. "Especially with the inclement weather on its way."

Monica looked at me. "Why is it that I feel a lecture coming on?"

We had been married long enough that she had called that ball correctly, so off I went.

"I get that they don't always listen and you have a lot going on, but if we take a moment to provide some background and explanation to them, then they'll learn and understand what's behind the ask, and hopefully learn to do it at some point without being asked."

"Oh, you think that would've solved the problem?"

"Better than 'because I said so.'" Checkmate!

Monica quickly came back at me.

"Well, 'because I said so' sounds pretty close to 'Hey, Dominic, that's enough questions.'"

I had overestimated my position, and the chess game continued. Monica's reference was to a recent exchange that I had with Dominic. As I've mentioned before, Dominic is our inquisitive one. "Why" may be his favorite word in the entire English language. The weekend before, while riding to Grandma's for dinner, I reminded Monica that we needed to select and purchase the items for the family we were adopting for Christmas, and reminded her that the kids needed to lead this endeavor. It was our way of teaching the children the importance of giving. I may have made the mistake of saying this in front of the kids without including them directly, because Dominic's "why?" flew in from the back seat.

Dale: "Why what, Dominic?"

Dominic: "Why are we adopting a family?"

Dale: "Because we are blessed, and it's important to give back."

Dominic: "Why?"

Dale: "First, it matches our value system of integrity and leadership, and also our faith."

Dominic: "But why is it important?"

Dale: "Because helping others is the right thing to do."

Dominic: "Why is it the right thing to do?"

Dale: "Because there are people who are less fortunate than us, we've been very blessed with what we've been given, and we want to help others."

Dominic: "I thought we did that already. We give at church."

Dale: "We do, Dominic, but around the holiday season it's important to make sure families enjoy the season as much as we do."

Dominic: "Why wouldn't they enjoy the season?"

Dale: "Dominic, you know why. That's enough."

At that point Dominic had beaten me down with his barrage of "why." I was happy that both Grant and Elizabeth had their headphones on and were listening to music and didn't get a chance to throw in their own "why."

So now it was checkmate for Monica. She continued.

"You know, Dale, if you had been specific about it and given the real 'why' – something like, 'They can't afford clothes or even a special meal because their bills go up during this time of year because gas for heating is more expensive, and they don't have extra money to just buy gifts' – then it would have worked better. I guess it's just like you told me 10 minutes ago: Specific examples are critical when teaching young children."

Talk about soapbox lectures! I felt like I was visiting the Twilight Zone. A few minutes before, I had the upper hand, chest out, having just taken care of a situation – and along comes Monica to deflate everything. I thought, *Teachers must go through this every day – kids walk up, figuring they caught their teachers in a mistake or an opportunity to show the teacher up a little, and the teacher turns it on them. The teacher gets the upper hand.* You would think by now that I would have wised up to that, but it wasn't the case.

The good news is there *was* a winner in our chess game, and that was our family. Monica and I spent time talking about the critical nature of "why" and the need to provide our kids with the rationale behind things we've asked them to do. Providing the "why" is powerful, because it provides understanding and clarity.

I watched Monica expertly apply her teachings just weeks later. One evening after dinner with Monica's parents, Elizabeth was putting away serving bowls and Monica asked her to put them in a different cabinet. Elizabeth quickly asked, "Why?" As Monica was giving her the "why," explaining that they have their place and it helps keep everything organized so when we need them next time we can find them, Monica was interrupted by Elizabeth's grandfather. "Elizabeth, don't question your mother. Just do what she tells you!"

Monica ignored her stepfather and continued with her explanation. "Elizabeth, everything has its place in the kitchen. It's your responsibility to put things where they belong, so they are available not only for you but for all of us. If you don't know where they go, just ask. Does that make sense?"

Elizabeth, who was standing attentively replied, "It does, Mom. Thanks." She finished her chore, and scurried off to do something else. Monica then turned teacher on her stepfather.

"Dale and I have come to the realization that giving the kids the 'why' helps them learn why we do things the way we do. Clarifying 'why' teaches them the knowledge to make decisions later. Taking responsibility reduces chaos and increases happiness. If you wouldn't mind, when you are asking them to do something, please tell them why. I think you'll find that it reduces the number of times you have to explain things."

I could tell by the look on his face that my father-in-law was stuck between the logic that Monica just shared and grief over the loss of "because I said so," one of his favorite lines. Interestingly, we have found that when we struggle with the "why," we have to question whether our request is aligned with our family values or whether we are just telling our kids, *I do enough for you. Now, you just do it.* Our values give us clarity, and our explanations as to "why" should match.

We also realized that it was important for us not to just "do it ourselves," because when we do that we strip from the kids the experience of doing things themselves. Giving them the "why" and letting them do the task is a great combination for learning and growing.

Purpose Not Perfection

The "why" question never seems to come at the right moment. We don't have the time or the emotional energy to sit and provide a reason. Additionally, we instinctively question whether our children are challenging our authority, or really looking to understand. Either way, we often turn and answer back the easiest thing to say: "Because I said so."

It is true that giving the "why" isn't always the most efficient way of accomplishing something, but it is frequently the most beneficial for our children and for our family's development. When kids understand why you have asked them to participate, they have the opportunity to take ownership of their actions. They are given the chance to learn and grow when they understand the "why."

We all know the day is coming when our children will walk out our door and into the world to fend for themselves. At that point, we need to have given them the love, education, and experiences to thrive on their own. The more "whys" we answer, the more likely that our kids will have the knowledge through understanding and experience to achieve their dreams.

We are our child's first and most important teacher. In everything we do, we are presented with the opportunity to expand their experience and knowledge. Embrace their questions, fulfill that curiosity, have a conversation, help them understand your perspective, and don't forget to understand theirs. *Why do you ask? What do you think?* Giving them the "why" enhances your culture of communication.

Give Them The 'Why'

They learn when they understand the "why"

The learning, experience, and knowledge is in the "why." Take the time to give it to them.

The better the understanding, the greater the chance of success – even with small tasks.

Yes, it takes more time

What takes more time now, will take less time later. The more they understand, the faster they will learn to do it themselves.

Do you know why?

When you can define and explain the "why" easily, then your explanation probably aligns with your family values and beliefs. If "because I said so" is your strongest defense, then you might want to spend some time reflecting on "why" yourself.

CHAPTER NINE

You Get What You Expect

First, have the right expectations. Then set and communicate them.

Imperfect Parenting

More frequent conversations with our kids gave us so many more opportunities to prove that we were imperfect parents. When we did something right, it was often apparent. But when we did something wrong, it was, well, glaring. One of those glaring moments was my attempt to instill Grant with confidence so he would succeed in his schoolwork. I thought all I had to do was set the expectation that "We believe in ourselves," and everything would work out. In hindsight, it's almost embarrassing to admit that I would set that expectation for an 8-year- old. What does "believe in yourself" even mean, anyway? How could I set an expectation around something Grant didn't know or understand?

It didn't turn out well. I was trying to get Grant to believe in himself when all around him people – his peers, and even at times his teachers – were sending him the message that there something wrong with him. He had no idea what I meant – and worse, all three kids feared that no matter what the topic, I would come back at them with a "believe in yourself" lecture. That was what Monica meant when she said I was scaring the kids. Again, in hindsight, it's pretty embarrassing to see how clueless I was.

So maybe the title of this chapter is not exactly what it seems. It is true that you get what you expect, but only if what you expect is within the realm of reason. Expectations are important, but what is critical is that we have the right ones to begin with. When I shared this latest epiphany with Monica, I learned that she was way ahead of me.

"Dale, I'm glad to hear you say that. That's exactly what bothered me when we started our family meetings. You expected the kids to sit through a long meeting, listen to your every word, and then instantly change the way they act. When they didn't respond the way you expected, you got frustrated with them. I was frustrated too – not at them, but at you. Your expectations were completely out of whack. I tried to tell you, but you weren't going to listen to anything that didn't fit your view of the world. You were pressing forward no matter what."

She was right. Instinctively I knew it, but I was convinced that if we pushed through the meetings, the kids would eventually get it. Monica had tried to explain to me that it wasn't likely to work that way, but we were seeing two different realities. I wanted the family meetings to be a success, so I had simply pushed forward.

I knew there had been no stopping me at that point, but I still couldn't resist asking.

"I guess there was really no way you could have stopped me, was there?"

"Oh, I tried," Monica quickly replied. "But you were going to hold those meetings the way you wanted come hell or high water. I told myself, just like I sometimes have to with the kids, *Be patient, provide gentle guidance, and wait for the realization to come on its own.*"

At that moment, I realized how difficult it could be to transfer professional leadership skills to your home and family. I think I run great meetings at work; I pride myself on how efficient and effective they are. The fact that the kids didn't instantly see the power of meetings wasn't their fault, but mine. The root of the problem was that my expectations weren't age-appropriate.

I nodded. I must admit that I truly appreciate Monica's ability to bring me back to reality with regard to parenting.

"Okay, I get it," I said. "I'm sorry I didn't get it sooner."

Monica laughed. "I'm glad you were a willing student today!"

"I'm always a willing student," I replied.

I thought we were done, but class was not over for the day. Monica must have sensed that she had fertile ground to work with. She continued.

"You know Dale," she said. "There is another side to this. The meetings aren't the only time that you have asked the kids, with little direction, to do things that they don't know how to do and don't understand what you expect. You imply your expectations, but they don't understand it. Then you get angry when things don't go well. You have to remember to make sure the expectations you set for the kids are appropriate in light of their age, skill level, and abilities."

Again, I knew she was right, but it wasn't easy to hear. I was feeling exasperated and wondering whether I was capable of being a competent parent. Monica must have sensed my despair, because she changed direction.

"Dale, you're not perfect, but you do a lot of things right, as well." The teacher was now going to lift up her student. "For example, you set the expectation with the kids that we were going to dress appropriately for church each Sunday. In that case, you gave them the expectation, you told them in great detail what was appropriate and in words they could understand, you showed them what it looked like, and you continued to encourage them to learn for themselves."

She's right, I thought. That was a great example of one thing we had done right and with great success. Monica and I set the expectation that everyone in the family should dress appropriately for church on Sunday as an affirmation of our respect for our faith. The kids would be happy to go in shorts and tennis shoes, but Monica and I felt that being appropriately dressed was important, and so it was collared shirts and long pants for the boys, a nice outfit for Elizabeth.

Both Monica and I made a point of dressing appropriately and discussed with the kids what they should wear. Frequently, one or more of them would attempt to slide one past us by getting in the car before we saw them or by running down the hallway late so we had no choice but to accept what they were wearing. This became a topic of one family meeting. We set the expectation, gave them the why, and then explained that we would rather be late for church than be inappropriately dressed. Dominic had difficulty understanding how being required to wear khakis and a collared shirt one day each week for an hour was *not* cruel and unusual punishment.

After a few weeks of gentle reminding and asking whether certain outfits were appropriate, the kids bought into our expectation, even to the point of self-policing!

One Sunday morning, I overheard Elizabeth in the kitchen saying to Grant, "I don't know, Grant. I don't think that shirt passes for church. I'd go change." Grant reluctantly went off to his room to change. As soon as he was out of sight, I rushed into the kitchen with my hand raised to deliver a high-five to Elizabeth.

I told Monica that I understood what she was saying about setting expectations, and was glad that we'd done so well with the "dressing for church" expectation. Assuming my lesson was over, I was ready to move on and spend some time reflecting on our conversation, something I frequently do after we have had a good discussion. Monica could see I was ready to take off and quickly said,

"Not so fast. We've got good momentum, so let's keep talking for five more minutes."

Monica was in full teacher mode and who was I to interrupt Mrs. Vernon? Monica explained that in the classroom, teachers try to set expectations that challenge children to reach a higher level of competence, but not so high that they lose interest or become overwhelmed by the challenge.

"Children who experience small successes will begin to crave bigger successes," she said. "None of this happens quickly but we are getting there. Just be patient. I'm proud of your willingness to change."

We agreed that we would set some expectations that pressed our kids beyond their comfort zone, but we had to be aware that this could also backfire on us if not used appropriately. And, of course, we still had to be clear about what we were asking. Monica ended our discussion with a big smile on her face.

"Class dismissed," she said, and I laughed, too. I had been pretty thoroughly schooled.

One expectation we set for the kids that really pushed them out of their comfort zone initially was the expectation that they introduce themselves to adults whom they meet for the first time. We set the expectation and taught the kids the following ways to behave:

- ✓ Look the other person in the eye.
- ✓ Introduce yourself with a loud enough voice to be heard.
- ✓ Shake their hand firmly.
- ✓ Repeat their name and tell them, "It's nice to meet you."

The instructions were simple, age-appropriate, and understandable, but still success didn't happen immediately. Monica and I had to give the kids a little nudge and say, "Introduce yourself, please." Then we had to provide small corrections along the way, reminding them, for example, to repeat the person's name.

Something happened over time. Their confidence grew. They became comfortable introducing themselves, and we praised them every time they did it. The more experience they had, the better they got at it. When we first set the expectation, we had to push the kids outside their comfort zone, but, in time, it became second nature for them.

Actually, I think the kids now truly enjoy meeting new people, because they love the reactions they get from adults and because their confidence has grown so much in doing so. A great example came one frigid winter day when Elizabeth and I were at a Cleveland Browns football tailgate. Prior to the game, she introduced herself to my friend's 30-year-old son. It was 26 degrees outside, and everyone was tightly bundled with gloves and hats. Elizabeth removed her glove, extended her hand, and introduced herself. My friend's son extended his gloved hand and while shaking it, stopped and said, "Oh you removed your glove. I should have done that. Sorry!"

Elizabeth beamed! She must have realized that she had just taught an adult something about manners. I had never set "remove your glove" as an expectation, but she had apparently been watching me.

When we started talking to the kids about expectations, we invited them to list their expectations for *us*. It seemed like a good way of emphasizing to them how important and serious we were about expectations. The expectations that they listed for us were interesting and thought-provoking:

- ✓ No yelling, not at them or at each other.
- ✓ Spend time with them just because we love them.
- ✓ Be willing to do things with them that they enjoy, even if we do not.

The last two expectations were especially meaningful. Sometimes you look forward to getting home from work and immediately heading outside to enjoy some extracurricular activities with the kids. Other times you are so thoroughly exhausted that all you want to do is collapse on the couch, even if it is to watch a re-run of *Criminal Minds* for the third time.

Dominic leverages the "I know you love me, Dad" card when he invites me to play a game of one-on-one kickball, even if I've just gotten home from work. How can I say no?

The most important expectations that we set for our kids are those that translate our family's values into our family's culture. They provide every member of the family with guidelines for putting our beliefs into action. These expectations say, "This is who we are, what we believe in, and how we live our life." One of ours is that we will communicate in our family, and that a one-word response is not communication. This expectation is borne of our commitment to our value of respect for each other. It helped create the foundation for a culture of communication.

Purpose Not Perfection

A part of every leader's responsibilities is to provide guidance to those he or she leads. This is true in business, in the military, in education, and most certainly in our families. One way we set direction is by setting expectations that drive the behavior we want to see.

Expectations benefit your children by giving them a sense of security and comfort – as long as what is expected is consistent and achievable. Therefore, the starting point must be to understand our children's capabilities so that our expectations are appropriate given their intellectual and physical skill levels.

Expectations that are beyond a child's current level of comfort can be beneficial, but can also be damaging. Setting expectations that are unattainable is setting your child and your family up for frustration, misery, and ultimate failure. Children tend to form beliefs about themselves based on the message they receive from us as parents. If your children fail to meet expectations, they will sense your disappointment and frustration no matter how hard you try to hide it, or they may just assume that they have disappointed you. We risk destroying their belief in themselves, because they realize they can't meet the expectations of Mom and Dad.

Setting expectations too low can also be damaging. A lot has been written about the current tendency to praise children in order to "build confidence," regardless of results. Thus, some advocate for not keeping score in youth games and giving every child a trophy for participating. Achievements that are gained without effort may increase a child's confidence in the short-term, but it does not teach the importance of hard work and effort in achieving success. If we don't expect much, we'll get what we expect – not much.

Seeing the potential in your children and believing in their ability to achieve that potential is critical. As Ralph Waldo Emerson said, "Treat a man as he is and he will remain as he is. Treat a man as he can and should be and he will become as he can and should be." Your children need to understand what is expected of them, and you need to have the right expectations for them.

You Get What You Expect

The role of the family leader: setting expectations

We get what we expect whether we realize it or not.

Set the direction: Be intentional and provide your family the guidance they need.

Have the right expectations

Set expectations for your children at a level that is attainable.

As they grow and their experiences grow, so should your expectations.

Clarity

Clear expectations provide your child with emotional security.

Clear expectations help build confidence in your kids, because they understand what is expected of them.

Treat your child as the person he or she will become.

CHAPTER TEN

Consistent & Continuous

Be continuous in what you do; be consistent in how you do it.

Imperfect Parenting

If parenting wasn't exhausting enough, trying to be consistent made it even more challenging. For us, being consistent meant implementing a number of changes in our family life at the same time. We pressed ahead with our family meetings and huddles, ignoring the kids' resistance to learning to listen and actively participate. We focused on responding, not reacting, meaning Monica and I had to break what had become a very strong habit of "instinctive" parenting. We avoided lectures and engaged in conversations, an activity that takes more time and patience than I could ever have imagined. We weaved explanations into nearly all of our directions and discussions with the kids, essentially giving them the "why" whether they asked for it or not. We continuously made reference to our family's values in setting expectations, in answering the "why," or in responding to an issue. In effect, we were introducing the kids to a new language and pushing them to think and act with that new language as a framework. Finally, we did our best to monitor and control our own behavior so that we were setting the best example possible. It was, for us, a lot of changes at one time.

Monica and I must confess that the effort to be aware of our every word and action made it seem like we were in a marathon with no finish line. It was very hard – at least at first. After a few months, we did learn that being consistent in our communication and parenting ultimately led to an easier home life for the entire family. "Easier" may not actually be the right word, but we certainly had a more rewarding, happy, and aligned family. We were growing stronger as a couple and closer as a family.

Thinking back to where we started, I realize now that we had paid a price in the past for being inconsistent. It's especially clear with respect to Grant's dyslexia. As I described earlier, Grant's struggles with homework were gut wrenching. He cried, Monica cried, and none of us knew what to do to fix things. Many nights we gave up while trying to manage Grant's struggles with homework, surrendering to his unhappiness and stress, and letting homework go incomplete. We used to do the same with Elizabeth and Dominic, as well. But what was hard to deal with one day only became harder the next day, for all of us. Incomplete homework has to be addressed along with new homework, and falling behind meant having to push harder to catch up.

Any behavior we let slide only got more difficult to correct, either because the kids weren't learning what our expectations were around the area of homework and education, or, worse, they were learning that we didn't really mean what we said. Early on with Grant, I would threaten him: "If you don't finish your homework, then you can't go over your friend's house and play." It was all bark with no bite. The homework didn't get done, and Grant was still permitted to go to his friend's house.

We ultimately learned that being consistent, although more difficult in the short-term, made life easier for everyone in the long-term. The expectation for homework in our house is now clear: Start your homework immediately after school. Do what you can on your own. Come to us for help when you need to. Get your homework completed and turned in on time.

All family relationships need consistency, and my relationship with Monica was no exception. Before we started to be intentional, there was no consistency as to how I was going to react (that's correct – not respond, but react) to Monica when she shared the day's issues with me. She never knew whether I was going to be a helpful resource and partner to address the issues she was facing with the kids, or if I was going to lose my temper, criticize, jump up on my soapbox, and chastise her for not managing a given issue. I eventually realized that my inconsistency was destroying any trust she had in me.

I learned to focus on being supportive, listening, and being a resource and good partner in helping manage the issues we faced. After all, the kids are *our* kids, not just her responsibility. Becoming consistent in my relationship with Monica led to the strong trust and stronger relationship we have today.

The benefit from being consistent and continuous is most apparent when someone in the family is struggling or facing a crisis. For example, we have consistently and continuously discussed the problem of bullying with the kids. Our first discussion took place when Elizabeth brought home a school pamphlet describing the school's anti-bullying campaign. As a teacher, Monica had seen firsthand the problems caused by bullying. We discussed with the kids why bullies do what they do and what was wrong with that kind of behavior. From time to time, if one of the kids was picked on or reported a friend being picked on, we would return to the earlier discussion. First and foremost, we did not want our kids to be bullies. Additionally, we wanted them to know how to respond if they were being picked on.

We saw the value of our consistent and continuous message on this topic when Grant was subjected to some ridicule during a school presentation. Incredibly, it took place right in front of Monica and me without either of us knowing about it. Grant and Dominic were participating in a robotics program at school. To prepare for a competition that was to take place the following weekend, all of the participants formally presented their projects to a group of parents and teachers. Each team prepared a PowerPoint presentation, and each member of the team took turns presenting, by reading from the presentation.

Like any parent, I worried how Grant would do. I was particularly concerned given his dyslexia. Reading is hard for him to begin with, and reading in public only added anxiety. I was concerned that the combination of the two was going to crush his confidence.

I was quite amazed by his performance. Grant not only spoke with confidence and a charisma that he had developed during the previous summer's drama camp, he also did it all in front of an audience of his peers and more than 20 adults. I thought it was quite courageous.

When he stumbled on the big words, his teammates helped him. It was great to see that support. During one part where he particularly struggled, he did something I thought took great character. He turned to the crowd and made a joke. "Man, I hate big words!" This got a chuckle from the audience.

A few moments later, as Grant continued and struggled with his portion of the presentation, a classmate in the front row said to him, "Apparently you don't like the small words, either." It was not audible enough for any of us to hear, but clearly loud enough for Grant.

I had arrived at the presentation from work, so we had two cars at the school. Elizabeth drove home with me, and the boys with Monica. I was unaware of what had transpired until we got home – and emotion and tension were high. Grant had shared with Monica what his classmate had said, and he was as upset as I had ever seen him. He flew through the door and blazed a trail to his bedroom, dropping his book bag and coat along the way.

I didn't have the full story, and only responded to the dropped coat and backpack. I called out, "Grant!"

He instantly shot back, "No, I don't want to talk about it."

I stood there confused, thinking, *Talk about what? Picking up the backpack?*

Monica walked in immediately thereafter and explained to me what had happened. We had had several conversations about bullies at that point, and I asked Monica if she had addressed the issue with Grant.

"I started to," Monica replied, "but he was so angry that I couldn't get a word in edgewise."

Before I could say more than, "Dear…" Monica interrupted me.

"Dale, don't you dare start. I know exactly what you are going to say, and I tried. You weren't there, so don't you dare judge how I handled this."

She was right; I was 100% judging her and her handling of this, but Monica did not want to hear anything from me. "Let it go," she said, and as soon as I took a breath, she repeated, "Dale, I said let it go."

I let it go with Monica, but I was bothered by the incident. It was clear that all Grant was focusing on was the negative and not all the positives from the evening. I did stop by Grant's room. He was hiding under his covers, as he always does when things really bother him. I started talking.

"Grant, I just wanted to let you know that I'm really proud of you and I love you." There was no response. Taking Monica's advice, I let it go, realizing that emotions were too high and this was an issue for tomorrow.

The next morning, I gave Monica a five-second heads up before the family huddle started that I was going to bring up last night's event. She quickly said, "I don't think that's a good idea."

Just as quickly, I said, "I do," and then immediately took over the start of the daily huddle in order to end our conversation.

"Okay, everyone: What went well yesterday and what didn't?" I looked over to the kitchen table where Grant sat with his blanket over his head. Without prompting, he yelled, "I don't want to talk about it." It was as if he said, *Yes Dad, I know you are trying to get me to discuss this.* Well, Grant is a kid with a lot of experience, especially when it comes to what to expect from me. He expected a conversation and that's exactly what was about to happen.

Monica looked at me and shook her head from side to side: *Don't do it; not now.*

It was clear that Monica and I were not in agreement, but I had no intention of stopping. We were a family that communicates, and there is no more critical time to be consistent than when facing a difficult conversation. It's important we teach our children that problems only get worse when we ignore them.

"Kids," I said, "I want to remind everyone that we are a family that communicates. We share positive things, and we share negative things. They are all opportunities for us to learn. But most importantly, we communicate."

Grant, knowing that my comment was directed at him, yelled from under his still head-covering blanket, "I don't want to talk about it."

I was ready for that response and said, "Grant, I understand you are upset, but as you know, we communicate in this family. We share our experiences for all to learn from. As difficult as this may be, and as upset as you may be, there is a lot of good to learn from your experience." I could see that this tack did not provide Grant the reinforcement I had hoped, so I pressed on in a slightly different direction.

"Why don't you want to discuss this?"

"Because I'm mad," Grant responded.

"Why?" I asked.

"Because he made me mad," Grant replied.

"Did anything good happen last night?" I asked.

Grant was starting to engage. "No. He made me mad and I wanted to punch him."

"But you didn't. You held your composure, and no one in the audience could even tell you were upset. That alone was positive." I decided to go on. "What else was positive?" I asked all the members of the family to participate.

Monica was ready to chime in and, I'm assuming, to help protect Grant. "I was proud of the fact that he stood in front of a room of people and read aloud and presented."

Elizabeth had shaken off the morning grogginess and chimed in. "He made a joke when he struggled with the big words. That was cool."

I was glad she jumped in. "Exactly, Elizabeth. Grant, you showed confidence and character when under pressure. That takes experience and you showed you had it."

My next question was to advance the theme around bullies, since we had a pretty consistent, ongoing discussion about this topic. I posed the question to the family: "Is this young man a bully?"

"Yes," Grant said. "He's a bully. He made me mad."

"Okay," I said. "This young man is a bully. What did he teach us?"

Dominic, who is usually the slowest to get going in the morning, said, "He's a bully."

Although Dominic was about a minute behind the conversation, I was glad he was taking part. "Dominic, thanks for participating. What makes him a bully?"

Grant was ready with the response. "He puts others down."

When I asked why, the responses came in rapid fire.

Elizabeth jumped in. "Because it lifts himself up and makes him feel better about himself when he puts others down."

Monica, realizing the conversation was going in a good direction, jumped in. "Why?"

Elizabeth was ready for the question. "Because he thinks he's better than you because he's good at something."

Monica was ready to advance the lesson. "And how should we feel about an individual like this?"

Grant, who was still upset, said, "We should feel sorry for them. They have to make fun of others to make themselves feel better."

Monica was now fully engaged. "Why?"

Dominic literally yelled, "Because we are positive – positiveness – and treat others the way we want to be treated."

I laughed. There was enthusiasm in the room and yelling at 6:08 in the morning.

Monica continued. "That's right. We feel badly for them. They pick on others to lift themselves up. We have positiveness as a family value. We lift others, we stand by those who struggle and help them because that's how we'd want to be treated. Bullies put others down, because they need to feel better about themselves. It's the only way they know how to make themselves feel good."

The only hang-up to morning huddles was time, so I wanted to advance the lesson. "So someone give me the positives."

Elizabeth volunteered. "Grant had courage. He read in front of people and did great."

"That's right, Elizabeth," I responded. "What else?"

Grant added, "The bully showed us how not to act and the wrong way to treat people."

"Grant, you got it," I responded. "Very good. How about the support your teammates gave you when you struggled? They supported you. That tells me that you've built trust with them. It's a relationship that says, 'We will help each other succeed.' That made me really proud."

Monica was right behind me. "I agree. Grant, you all did a great job. Speaking in front of people is not easy."

At this point we were more than out of time and I needed to wrap things up.

"So, we know what bullies look like. They put others down to lift themselves up. But we should feel sorry for them, because it's the way they make themselves feel better. We don't behave like bullies. As a matter of fact, we feel sorry for people that do, because they don't believe in themselves enough or know who they are, so they can't be positive influences or lead others in good ways. We have the courage to be the person we want to be, and in the end, we will not let bullies control us. Everyone, great job today. Now before we wrap up, what's on the agenda for the day?"

I was so thrilled! Our consistent and continuous conversation about bullies had sunk in. Bullies are inevitable, and being a kid means that everyone is angling to be cool and part of the "in group." Now we saw our kids becoming comfortable with who they were, fitting in where they wanted to, not forcing themselves to be someone who does something because that is what the "cool" kids do.

We could have easily skipped the conversation that morning, and we could have assumed one discussion with the kids about bullies was enough. But here is what we've learned: There are no quick answers to life's occurrences and no quick fixes to our children's problem and obstacles. What we do know is that we *have to* be consistent and continuous in how we respond to them. It would have been easier to avoid the conversation, especially for Grant, but avoiding it would have repudiated the culture of communication that we are developing in our family.

Over time, our kids have learned that they should focus on solving problems and addressing struggles by looking to our family's values. Because we consistently and continuously discuss those values, they now readily understand positiveness, helping others, respect, leadership, and courage. Everyone faces bullies from time to time, but when you can face them knowing who you are, what you believe, and how you do things differently, it gives you the experience and confidence to do so.

That day went from great to amazing for me when Monica and I discussed the morning's events that night. Monica said to me, "It's hard for me to press these issues, when I see Grant or any of them hurting, and I didn't want to force the conversation."

I hugged her. I can always tell when Monica wants a hug. She walks toward me without extending her arms, looks up at me with a look that says, *Please hug me.* I did, and she continued. "Dale, doing what is right is difficult."

"Dear, they are lucky to have a mother who cares and loves them so much."

She pulled away from the hug, looked at me, and returned the compliment.

"No Dale, it's you they are lucky to have. You've pushed all of us, and at times too hard, but conversations like the one this morning ... I couldn't, I mean, we wouldn't have gotten here without you." She paused for a moment and continued. "You know when we started the family meetings, I hated them. But I knew that if we didn't do them, it would only create more tension in our marriage. I knew you were doing them because you cared. I wanted to give up and you wouldn't let us, and now they make us so much better. You are unwavering. I admire your consistency and passion for our family."

After a long pause, Monica continued, "We are a much happier family and we are a much better couple. Thank you."

Wow! Her affirmation convinced me that we were on the right path. I just held her and thought about how far we had come as a couple and as a family. Our being consistent and continuous was paying off and making us so much more successful as parents.

Purpose Not Perfection

The consequences of inconsistently applying discipline are self-evident. Children readily push boundaries to see what they can get away with and are more likely to repeat misbehavior that goes unchallenged by one or both parents. Over time this can create confusion as to what is right and what is wrong – whether certain behavior really is unacceptable.

At times, this lack of predictability and reliability can create anxiety and confusion for our children. If you don't believe this, think about a relationship you have, perhaps with a colleague at work or another family member, where you feel like you are always "walking on eggshells" around that person. Why is that? More than likely, it is because you don't know how that individual will react to a given situation. That individual's inconsistency is creating your anxiety.

Our consistency and continuity builds and strengthens our children's trust with us. They develop the comfort of knowing what to expect of us and what we expect of them. They can rely on how we will communicate with them, how we will respond to their concerns, and that we will support them in times of need.

One of the reasons to emphasize a culture of communicating through family values is that it provides a consistent and continuous language and framework for expectations. The family values become a reference point for each member of the family. They help assure a consistent and continuous message from which children can learn how to deal with life's problems.

Consistent & Continuous

Be intentional

Intention on your part transfers to quick understanding on your children's part.

Be predictable

Predictability builds comfort and trust, because your children know what to expect.

Predictable routines increase your probability of success

Be a family that communicates

Being consistent and continuous as a family that communicates builds the framework to address issues and build family unity.

Action

*Turn Effort Into Experiences
and Confidence*

CHAPTER ELEVEN

Let Them Do It

Experience builds knowledge, knowledge builds confidence,

and confidence builds everything else.

Imperfect Parenting

We are all simply the product of a series of life experiences. Because Monica and I were in our mid-30s before we came to grips with our imperfect parenting ways, we each had 35 years of baggage and bad habits that we had to rethink. Through focused effort, we forced ourselves to break bad habits and learn to do things differently. With some things, such as using our values as a common language, we were learning brand new skills. At times, it was difficult. But, as with everything else, once you've done it for a while, your experiences build upon each other and, sooner or later, the behavior becomes second nature – it becomes a part of who you are.

One parenting habit that we struggled to break was doing things for our children as opposed to letting them do things for themselves. For Monica, her maternal instincts have driven her to take care of her babies from the time they were newborn to today. It seems that she lives primarily to take care of them and do things for them; I think they will always be her babies! For me, it is often just easier to do things myself than take the time to teach the kids to do something or wait for them to complete something that I could complete in a tenth of the time.

I knew this was an area where we could improve. As a kid, I had learned to do things myself. My dad worked seven days a week, and my mom had five other kids who needed her attention. Learning by doing was a matter of necessity in our household, and I was proud of my self-reliance. I wanted my children to feel that same sense of satisfaction. For that reason, I found it easier than Monica to embrace the idea of letting the kids do things for themselves, and it was easier for me to force myself to step back even when my instinct was to just do whatever needed to be done.

For Monica, doing less for those you love was like learning to write with the opposite hand: beyond difficult. Besides, she was an only child, with a very caring and loving mom who loved to do things for her, so she had the model of a mother who would always swoop in to make things easier. She wasn't convinced that this was an area where we needed work and we often squabbled over it – Monica doing things for the kids and me arguing for her to stop.

Ironically, Monica finally embraced the value of letting our kids do things for themselves when she observed a friend doing too much for hers. We were out to dinner one evening with another family – Jennie, her husband, and their two children, ages 8 and 10.

We learned early on that a restaurant was a good place for the kids to learn to communicate with adults. We established the expectation that the kids should read the menu for themselves, address any questions about the menu to the server rather than to us, and order their own meals. If the server asked a question like, "Would you like French fries or fruit with that?" they would have to think for themselves and respond.

While Monica embraced the expectation, she often would answer, "Fruit," before the kids had a chance to respond. After frequent reminders to let the kids come to their own conclusions about what to order, she would bite her lip, but you could tell how difficult it was for her to stay silent while our children worked through it, listening, thinking, and responding to an adult with whom they were unfamiliar. She wanted them to jump right to the "right" answer, so she provided it for them instead of letting them choose, and, perhaps, choose in a way she did not approve of.

This particular evening, the waitress approached Jennie's children to take their order first. Jennie did all the talking for her kids. When the waitress asked a question, the kids just sat quietly with blank stares on their faces, and Mom took care of everything. If that wasn't enough, when the food came, Mom cut the hamburger and sliced up the chicken fingers for her kids, who were the same ages as Elizabeth and Grant. When it was time for our kids to order, they handled themselves differently by owning the experience, and they wielded their own utensils.

By the time we got to the car, Monica could hardly wait to comment. "Dale, did you notice Jennie tonight?"

"What do you mean?" I asked.

"She did everything for her kids," Monica replied. "It was like she didn't even let them think. She did everything."

I was excited that Monica had picked up on this, but I had to be careful with my response. The "old Dale" (as Monica calls him) would have responded sarcastically, perhaps with a "Duh!" But the new Dale recognized a teachable moment – for Monica. So I resisted my urge to be sarcastic and responded to her question with a question of my own.

"So why is that a big deal?"

Monica was absolutely unaware that I knew exactly what she was talking about. "Well, if she does everything for them, how are they going to learn to think and communicate, especially in public? You can't speak for your children forever. They have to learn to have their own voice and learn to respond and communicate beyond texting. It's part of learning to be independent."

I was truly enjoying Monica's "aha" moment, and I tried to hide it. Unfortunately, I must have smirked and exposed myself, because after a few seconds of silence, Monica said, "Oh my God, of course you noticed!" With a slight pause, she continued. "Don't you dare say it!"

This was too much fun for me not to say something, so I responded, "Say what?"

Monica surrendered. "This is what you've been telling me all the time about doing things for the kids." I was now smiling from ear to ear, but I stayed silent to let Monica's self-provided lesson sink in.

Monica broke the moment, "You are such an ass!" But this time, she said it with a smile. I think she appreciated that I did not get sarcastic or get on my soapbox, but instead allowed her time to reflect on her own insights and experiences.

Not one to leave well enough alone, I still found a way to get into trouble. "So, this is what you do as a teacher with your students, huh? Let them teach themselves when you know they have the answer by just asking questions?"

She smiled and in her loving way said, "Oh, shut up!" as we both laughed.

For me, the hardest lesson in "letting them do it" is when something in the house needs to be fixed or assembled. I know the kids should participate to learn how to think critically and use a hammer, screwdriver, and other tools – to gain experiences – but it's so difficult to watch them struggle.

One Christmas, the kids' grandfather purchased a TV stand for their game room. I stared at the box, thinking, *I can get this done in 20 minutes if no one bothers me. However, if I do that, I'm stripping my children of an experience and opportunity and that isn't worth saving time.* I brought the kids together and explained to them what "we" were going to do. I was surprised that I only had 30 seconds of resistance before they said, "Okay Dad, let's get it done."

An hour and a half later, we placed the TV on the stand. The lessons learned were invaluable. I gently guided them as they struggled with the directions and which tools to use. At one point, we had a five-minute conversation about flat-head versus Phillips head screwdrivers. Five minutes, think about that! Well, at least I am now confident they will never get the two mixed up.

Sometimes, the best reward for "letting them do it" is being there to watch and hear them interact. As we assembled the TV stand, Elizabeth looked at two pieces of wood that were slightly askew and said, "I don't think this is aligned." Without pause, Dominic grabbed a hammer, hit the stand once with a good swing and said, "Now it is." I laughed, thinking that it must be a male gene thing.

Six weeks later, I came home to find Grant's room in total disarray. He was in the process of assembling a bookcase and a desk that Monica had purchased for him, and parts were everywhere. I asked him if he needed my help and he answered, "Nope. I got it." I reflected on the power of "teaching them to fish," and I left him to his project. A day and a half later, Grant had not only assembled his desk and bookcase, but had them neatly organized with all of his things.

"Letting them do it" also means encouraging our children to think critically for themselves rather than allowing them to simply ask questions and get an answer from us without applying any thought to it. As I mentioned earlier, Dominic loves to ask questions. Sometimes the questions reflect his curiosity, but other times they reflect an unwillingness to engage in hard thinking. It's taken time, but Monica has gotten really good at answering those questions with, "Well, what do you think, Dominic?" This has been a struggle for Monica. Her normal reaction would be to answer the question and move on, but, like everything else we've been intentional about, over time she slowly chipped away at her imperfect way and found the benefit of letting the kids do it themselves. She realized the importance of helping them be independent.

Examples of parents *not* "letting them do it" are all around us. As we were in the middle of writing this book, we were out with our friends Rick and Amy, and talking about family and kids. Somehow the topic of organization came up. Rick told a recent story about Amy scrambling to keep their fifth-grade son organized by "doing it for him." Rick, wanting to give credit where credit was due, told her, "You are really doing great work as a fifth grader." That was Amy's light-bulb moment.

Monica and I smiled at each other, knowing that we were thinking the same thing. We weren't judging. As a matter of fact, we think of such moments as reminders about what we need to do in our family. Letting them do it and letting them participate in doing something is at times inconvenient and far more difficult than just doing it ourselves or for them, but that is in the short-term. In the long-term, who our children become is derived from their experiences, and we owe it to them to give them as many experiences as possible.

Purpose Not Perfection

Think about something you know how to do, something simple like putting gas in a car or ironing a shirt. How did you learn how to do it? Was it by watching someone do it for you or was it by doing it yourself? Even though we learn some things by watching others, we learn most effectively how to do things by doing them. The more we perform a task or a skill, the more experience we gain, and the more confidence we have in our ability to execute that task or skill.

Early in our children's lives, we take great joy in watching them learn to do things for the first time, whether it's taking the first step or learning to hold a spoon and feed themselves. They learn not by solely watching us, but by doing it themselves. We embrace the concept of learning by doing. As our children get older, however, we have to ensure that we continue to provide them opportunities to gain experiences and learn to do things for themselves. It might be easier or quicker now to do it for them or make decisions on their behalf, but when we do that, we are stripping our children of teachable moments and the opportunity of experience.

Don't lose sight of the fact that there are opportunities every day to allow our children to learn by experience. Whether it is having them handle chores on their own, assisting you in a home repair or home improvement project, planning a trip, ordering food at a restaurant, carrying on a conversation with an adult, helping organize a party, or solving a problem on their own, your child can learn by doing or by helping. All that is needed is for you to invite your child into the experience.

The same goes for problem-solving. If your child comes to you to solve a problem, you need to decide what gift you will give them. It's either the gift of dependence, because you solve the problem for them, or the gift of independence, because you encourage them to work through a solution themselves.

Experience in life is critical. It is ultimately the only thing that builds confidence. We are all a series of our experiences, so give your children the gift of independence and let them do it.

Let Them Do It

Experience – confidence

We learn when we do. Give your children a chance to learn by doing.

Confidence comes from our experiences. The more experiences mean the more knowledge we gain. The more knowledge, the more confidence your children will build in themselves.

We are all a series of our own experiences and have learned through all of them, good and bad. Help your kids gain experiences small and large.

Take the time to teach.

Fail your way to success

Teach your children to take the first step. A willingness to fail means the willingness to learn and grow.

Failing is a learning experience. Even when we fail, we gain knowledge and experience.

Let them fail and you let them grow.

Stop it – bite your tongue

Let them answer for themselves.

Imagine the day you are not there for them.

CHAPTER TWELVE

Effort Is My Smart

Through effort we find success. Develop a growth mindset.

Imperfect Parenting

As we've shared our journey throughout this book, you have probably noticed that we've had more than a couple life-changing moments. Many of those moments have become a permanent part of who we are today. Nothing was more impactful than hearing Grant say, "Dad, you don't get it. I'm the stupid kid." It launched our mission to help our children succeed, although we didn't know exactly where we were going or how we were going to get there. We only knew that failure was not an option.

Our journey started falsely with my idea that teaching our children confidence could solve all of their problems. That failure led to an endless search for answers – at times we found answers to questions that we didn't even know we had.

It was all beginning to evolve positively on the home front, but there was still the nagging reality around education that kept us unsettled mentally and emotionally. Grant, and to a lesser extent Elizabeth and Dominic (who also have dyslexia, although a milder form), continued to struggle at school. We seemed powerless to help them.

The searching paid off when we stumbled upon the theory of a growth mindset. It was at that moment that everything we were doing became clear. Our efforts crystallized into something solid, something that we could not only wrap our heads around but effectively use within our culture of communication to help our kids academically. Learning about the concept of a growth mindset was inspirational.

We were camping with friends at a family campground 40 minutes from home, just west of the Ohio-Pennsylvania border. It was cool when I walked out of the camper around 6:25 a.m. I love the smell of a campfire, so I refreshed the one from the night before. I started the coffee and settled into a chair to review the news of the day on my iPad. (Yes, cushy chair and iPad. We were not exactly roughing it, sleeping in a fifth wheel camper with plenty of storage and access to the Internet via mobile technology.)

After 15 minutes of reviewing local and national news websites, I began a Google search. I often do this to see where it might take me, to see what I might learn. That morning, I started a Google search with the phrase, "How to raise smart kids." I had no doubt searched similar phrases before, but I must never have used that one, or perhaps I never paid attention. The third resource listed was a headline from *Scientific American* titled, "The Secret of Raising Smart Kids" by Carol Dweck, Ph.D. I clicked on it. The teaser caught my attention. It was a story about a student named Jonathan who had easily sailed through school for many years but suddenly lost interest in academics. As he started to struggle, his parents tried to bolster his confidence by assuring him that he was smart. It didn't work.

I paused. *Wait,* I thought, *that's what we are doing, and, no, it wasn't working for us, either!* Grant was making progress at school, but we were concerned whether it was going to be enough long-term. After this year, we knew a decision had to be made about whether to keep Grant where he was, which required his going to the upper school, or moving him to another school, where he could take more time to master fundamental skills. We struggled. *If we decided to change schools again, would this hurt Grant's progress? Could we find a school that would meet his needs? Could Grant do just as well in a regularly paced classroom?* I had to read more. I clicked through to the full article and was introduced to the concept of a growth mindset.

According to Dr. Dweck, who is a professor of psychology at Stanford University, people with a fixed mindset believe that their basic qualities, such as intelligence or talent, are simply fixed traits. They also believe that talent alone creates success, and not effort. People with a growth mindset, on the other hand, believe that their most basic abilities can be developed through hard work and effort. They embrace the challenge of finding a solution and view challenges and failures as opportunities to learn and gain new skills.

Dr. Dweck's research has shown that kids who are praised for their intelligence, over time tend to shy away from challenges. If they encounter difficulty, they are inclined to want to quit. Their behavior suggests that they don't want to put the past praise at risk by failing to live up to that praise. If, however, parents praise a child's *process* – their strategies, effort, and their perseverance – then the child learns that *those* are the ingredients of success. These children are not afraid of failing. They are not intimidated when things get harder; they simply engage more deeply in the process of learning.

I thought, *How is it that I've been searching the Internet and other resources for more than three years and I'm only now finding this?* This wasn't new material. Dr. Dweck had published this theory nearly a decade earlier. But it was exactly what I needed: a scientific, unified explanation of how to help a child succeed in school and in life. It felt like I'd found the Holy Grail!

I read the article three times. Then I started jotting down key words like "effort" and "process praising," all ways to help a child realize that it's the process of finding a solution and not the end result that matters.

I couldn't wait to share this information with Monica. By the time she woke up and settled into her chair by the campfire, I launched into what I had found. I must have caught her off guard because she peered at me and asked, "Exactly how many cups of coffee have you had this morning?"

"Five," I replied, "but that's not important. Do you realize what this means?"

Monica and I discussed Dr. Dweck's research for the next half an hour and she slowly began to see the significance of what the growth mindset theory could mean for our family.

Our family camping trip was saved by the fact that I didn't have the bandwidth to download a book – but the moment I got home, I ordered Dr. Dweck's *Mindset: The New Psychology of Success,* and read it straight through. I asked Monica to read it, too.

After finishing the book, Monica and I had many long discussions about the science and implications of Dr. Dweck's work and what it could mean for our family. We decided to start immediately praising our kids' efforts rather than their smarts, and it was as if all our efforts with the kids were suddenly amplified.

We were amazed, when we started paying attention, at how often we said, "Good job. You are smart." It turned out that we often said it about ourselves, too. I would do something like fix a broken toy for the kids, and they would say, "Wow, Dad, how do you know how to do that?" Instead of talking about experiences, effort, and seeking a solution, I'd simply say, "Because I'm smart." Apparently, I was humble as well. We had to remove the "you are smart" demon from the Vernon vocabulary and household. It was a tough habit to break, but we had to do it.

The kids responded positively to being praised for their efforts and in a very short time developed a new attitude toward their schoolwork and every other challenge they faced. They became more willing to do things on their own and became less discouraged when faced with difficult tasks.

We eventually made the decision to bring Grant back to a local school. When we told him of our decision, his response shocked us. Grant approached Monica the next day and told her that he wanted to repeat the sixth grade at the new school instead of moving into the upper school. When Monica asked him why, he simply said, "Because it will give me a better chance."

I shared with Grant that kids would ask about the age difference and why he was now in the same grade as his sister. "Dad, I'll just tell them I have a learning disability and that it helped me to take an extra year. It will be fine." Grant's response showed the maturity of an adult. It was proof to us that all the different parts of what we were doing were starting to come together. We believe the combination of our culture of communication and his newfound growth mindset was the reason Grant was comfortable making his decision.

Part of developing a growth mindset is learning to try new things and being willing to fail. To grow, you must be willing to take that first step. By taking the first step, you begin the journey to a solution and gain experience. The effort of finding a solution translates into experience and knowledge. This is the mindset that leads to confidence, but not all experiences are successful. Failure is an inevitable part of the learning process. If you have a growth mindset, all experiences, even failures, provide you with knowledge that can be used to find the right solution in the future.

Grant's experience with rappelling provides a good illustration of how a growth mindset can help build confidence. His Boy Scout troop had scheduled their annual rappelling trip, which included both an 80-foot and 175-foot drop. Grant made it clear to me that he had no interest in going on the trip. "It scares me," he repeated any time the topic was raised.

"Grant, how do we make something less scary?" I asked. I then answered my own question. "We do it." I remember thinking I would have handled this much differently and more aggressively before learning of Dr. Dweck's work.

"Dad, I'm scared because I've never done it before."

"Exactly!" I responded. "Do you trust your scout masters and their experience?"

Grant replied, "Of course."

"Great, then how do we learn how to do something we are scared of in order to build our understanding of it?"

Grant was following the logic, "We try it."

"Exactly!" I replied again. "It's always scary when you don't know, but when you look for solutions and you are willing to try, that is when the learning begins."

It took a couple of weeks of similar conversations, but Grant and I ultimately agreed that he'd go rappelling if I went too.

The weekend trip was scheduled to begin Thursday as opposed to the normal Friday night, because the boys did not have school on Friday. Since I had to work that day, I told Grant that I would reach the camp by nightfall and we could do our rappelling on Saturday.

By the time I arrived at the campsite, Grant couldn't wait to share his experiences with me. Not only had he tried rappelling, he went down the side of the cliff five times. He loved it, and he promised to show me how to rappel the next morning. As I had learned from Dr. Dweck's work, I praised him for his effort, and his willingness to take the first step. Grant found a solution that gave him the confidence he needed to rappel. I made sure he knew that I was very proud of him.

I asked one of the scout masters how he had gotten Grant to participate.

"Grant told me that you would make him try tomorrow, and he wanted to do it on his terms and at his pace. Grant watched a number of the other kids go down the cliff, and then he tried it."

I realized all of our conversations about taking the first step, finding solutions, and effort where paying off.

The next day, I was surprised and delighted to see Grant instructing other scouts and tying harnesses. It was as if he had become an expert in one day, by building his own confidence through his experience. I trusted that very experience as he tied my harness. I carefully watched as he checked to make sure his 210-pound dad was strapped in correctly. When he was finished, one of the certified instructors looked over his work, gave a thumbs up of approval, and said, "You are ready to go."

I gained even greater respect for my son when I found myself leaning backwards over an 80-foot cliff, relying on Grant's coaching. "Look forward, Dad, and keep leaning backwards." It was a scary experience! I knew one thing, though: I had to do this and be the example of what I had been preaching to Grant over the last several months.

When I reached the bottom, my fear now gone, Grant was already there to meet me. With a high-five he asked, "How was it?"

I replied, "Awesome" and quickly told him that I couldn't have done it without him showing me how. We both went down several more times, including the 175-foot drop later that day.

Unquestionably, teaching our children to have a growth mindset is the single most important change around their education and mindset we have made in our child-rearing. We encourage our children to take the first step, to try to learn things or do things, and if, by chance, we hear, "I can't!" then Monica and I are quick to follow with a "Yet." We don't criticize failure but encourage the kids to learn from their effort. One of our favorite expressions is "effort is your smart," meaning you learn by trying and gaining experience. In seeking a solution, you will gain experience, you will improve, and, eventually, you will succeed. Grant and I both learned that lesson on the rappelling trip.

An incident that occurred during the writing of this book convinced me that our efforts to build confidence by encouraging a growth mindset were working. Seven years into our new journey, almost to the week that those catalytic words left Grant's mouth, we lost Monica's father at the young age of 63. He had fought a long battle with cancer, and we were blessed to have him with us for that last Christmas in 2014. He passed the day after, on Dec. 26. One of the most difficult moments we've had as parents was breaking the news of his passing to our children and answering their many, many "whys."

However, from this deep moment of sorrow came one of our proudest moments. The four-hour wake was held the day before the funeral. When it ended, we returned home, and Monica and I started a fire and sat down to relax and talk. Dominic, who was now 12 years old, walked in and announced to us that he wanted to speak at the funeral. Since it was Monica's father, I sat silently and looked for her to take the lead.

Monica was exhausted, but she didn't let that prevent her from encouraging him.

"Dominic, I'm okay with that, and I'm proud of you for your courage. But I want you to write it out first and then practice it."

Dominic was excited, "Great! Thanks Mom!"

But Monica wasn't finished. "Hold on, how long do you plan on speaking?"

Dominic was ready for the question. "I want to talk for two minutes."

At this point, I felt the need to intervene,. "Dominic, I'm proud of you, but I need to invoke some fatherly wisdom and suggest you write about 30 seconds of what you want to say. It may take you two minutes to say it, Buddy."

With that, Dominic said, "Okay," and rushed off to write and practice.

The next morning I asked him about what he wanted to say and if he was ready. He was all set.

"Mom and I went through it and talked about it, and I've practiced. I'm ready to go."

At that point, I abandoned my concern. I was proud of what he was doing.

Later that morning, about a hundred people gathered at the funeral home for the ceremony. Dominic was seated to my right and Grant to my left. Elizabeth was a couple of chairs down, sitting between her cousins. Monica was in front of us with her stepmother and half-brothers. During the service, and after Monica had gotten up to say some wonderful words about her father, I realized that emotion had overcome Dominic and he might not want to read his speech. I leaned over to encourage him.

"Dominic, there is nothing to be afraid of. Grandpa is proud of you no matter what." I paused for a moment, partially because I was talking during the middle of the service, and then I leaned back over and asked, "Do you still want to speak?"

Dominic's eyes were full of tears, and he shook his head, *No.* I paused for a moment, collected my thoughts, and leaned back again. "Do you want me to read it for you?"

Without pause, he handed me his speech and nodded, *Yes.*

"I'm happy to do it," I told him, "and I'm proud of you for writing it."

Grant must have been paying attention and realized something was up, because he leaned toward my left ear and asked, "Is Dominic going to get up and speak?"

I said no. Immediately, I felt Grant snag Dominic's speech from my hand and say, "Dad, I got it."

I was so proud of both of my boys, one for having the courage to write and want to say something at his grandfather's funeral, and the other for standing up for his brother in a moment of need. I guess our family value of courage had taken hold. I knew my father-in-law would be proud of them, as well.

This moment proved that our efforts had been working, because the "stupid kid" was about to get up and shock everyone in the service who knew about him and his learning difficulties. He was the same kid who months earlier was mocked by another student in front of others for "not liking small words either."

The minister was about to conclude the service, so I raised my hand and gestured that Grant wanted to say a few words. The minister invited him up.

Grant walked to the lectern and unfolded Dominic's speech, a speech that he had not even seen. He proudly began, "This is a letter from my brother, Dominic, to my grandfather. 'I remember many things about my grandpa. The one thing I will miss most about him was his voice. He used to use his voice and make it sound like Donald Duck. It always made me laugh. Another thing I remember is my grandpa always knew the right things to say to me if I was sad. He didn't even have to ask me what was wrong. Grandpa just knew what words to say to make me feel better. I miss you, Grandpa, and will always remember you.'"

When Grant finished, he started folding the paper and, with the confidence and experience of someone who has given a countless number of speeches, continued: "I would also like to say that I'm happy for my grandfather. I know he is in a better place. I would like to thank all of you for joining us today. Thank you."

I was shocked, stunned, and in awe. This was my son, the one who had been mocked, ridiculed, and bullied any time he spoke in front of others? I was crying. Well, I had already been crying, but now my tears were that of a proud father. My brothers and sisters, other family, and friends who were there to support Monica made countless comments to us about Grant's speech. It was so clear that our efforts were paying off. What a fitting tribute it was to a grandfather who believed in family, effort, courage, and experience. There is no question their grandfather was proud of them that day, proud of both of them! Proud of not only their actions, but also of the young men they were becoming and the men they would be.

Our journey wasn't simply about creating confidence in our children, but about giving them experiences and building the right mindset for their life's journey. Would we have gotten to this point without learning about a growth mindset, the importance of effort, taking the first step, and learning through experience? I don't know, but it doesn't matter, because we did and it's changed everything. Dr. Dweck's model of the growth mindset provided us with the missing piece of the puzzle to help our family succeed.

Purpose Not Perfection

There is a Nike commercial featuring Michael Jordan called, "Maybe It's My Fault." In it, a man who is arguably the greatest basketball player to ever play the game tells us that maybe it's his fault that he's led us to believe that he had "God-given talent" or that it was easy for him. He reminds us of what it really takes to succeed in life.

Our society, however, worships talent, not effort. Many people incorrectly assume that possessing superior intelligence and ability is what makes others successful. We know this is not true. Success and greatness happen primarily as a result of effort, perseverance, and experience.

A fixed mindset teaches that intelligence and ability are something that we either have or don't have. Children who develop a fixed mindset will stop trying when they have difficulty doing anything, because they have come to believe that talent is innate, not developed. In fact, they may become discouraged or even feel stupid if they encounter difficulty. A fixed mindset creates limitations and sets a child up for failure, because effort is not at the foundation of their learning.

The principal of a growth mindset asserts that our most basic abilities can be developed and enhanced through continuous effort and the process of finding solutions and learning from failures. Our brain grows stronger through seeking the pieces of the puzzle, and finding the solutions to a problem. Effort and learning through failures are the keys to lifelong learning.

Remember, we are our children's first and most important teachers. We ourselves must develop a mindset philosophy and provide the powerful example our children need.

One of the most difficult concepts for kids to grasp is that failure provides experience and knowledge. If we are to develop a growth mindset in our children, we must focus our attention – and our praise – not on the end result, but on the efforts our children are making to achieve the result, whether those efforts are successful or not. This is the essence of "process praising." We are encouraging our children to learn by taking the first step and doing, in order to gain experience. The end result is less important.

A good way to teach a growth mindset is to develop a concept of "yet" in your home. "I don't understand – yet" and "I can't do that – yet." It is a good way of driving the momentum of a growth mindset in your family and reminding your children that learning and achieving success in any venture requires effort, practice, and sometimes failure.

Experience is what builds confidence. That was our epiphany. I started our journey by trying to figure out how to teach confidence. What I learned was that you *can't* teach confidence. Instead, you can help children gain it through their experiences. Without experience and the risk of failure, we can't possibly build the confidence we need to succeed in our given fields.

By now you must be thinking, "This can't be easy." Change never is, but you have to work hardest for what you love most. Changing the way you think, communicate, and act is the first step. Remember, even for you as parents, "effort is my smart."

Effort Is My Smart

Growth mindset

Be the example of a growth mindset – live your life with one. You are your child's first and most important teacher, you are the example.

Praise the process – the effort your child makes to find a solution.

Where you used to say "you are smart," now say "effort is your smart."

EPILOGUE

By Monica Vernon

First, we would like to thank you for letting us share our story with you. Even though our journey started because of our son's learning disabilities, we found that our struggles were not significantly different than those of many other families.

It may seem like this all happened in an orderly manner, with wisdom unfolding before us in some logical fashion. There could be nothing further from the truth. When Dale determined that he needed to help Grant and our family, he attacked the problem with an extraordinary intensity, reading and outlining books, filling journals with notes and ideas for developing a successful and happy family. I resisted some of Dale's ideas and accepted others. Not all of the ideas we embraced were the right fit for our family, but we couldn't know that until we tried to implement them.

Over time, we realized that there was plenty of information available that described what should be done to address a particular problem. As Dale has said, our struggle was not managing all the "what" we learned and uncovered. We struggled with the "how" – how to implement all the things we had learned and wanted to do for our family in a practical and effective way. We ultimately ended up with the framework that we've shared in this book: The "how" that ultimately defined *who we are, what we believe in,* and *how we do it.*

Our journey, like the journeys of so many other families, was full of valleys and hilltops, tears and laughter, arguments and hugs. What kept us together and kept us going was our love for each other and our love for our children. We just had to find a way – a way to be a better, happier family, a way to be *us* individually but stronger together.

We can say with 100% confidence that the events described in the chapter, "Together Stronger," are what changed everything. For us, someone had to go first. Dale realized one day that he was the one who had to take the first step. I am blessed to have married a man who was willing to look in the mirror, be self-critical, and put his family in front of himself. Somehow, whether by reflection, divine intervention, or whatever you want to call it, he realized what needed to be done. He had the strength and courage to accept that what needed to be fixed most started with him. He was willing to admit, "I'm imperfect, and I need to change." He was willing to change whatever was necessary in order to have a better family.

Our first conversation was not easy. I was not prepared when he asked me to tell him what he was doing wrong and needed to do differently. I was not prepared to tear down the man I loved. Yes, he drove me crazy at times with his ideas, long work hours, and impatient demands for change in our home and family. Many times, I thought life would be easier if he just wasn't around. But I loved him – I had since the 11th grade – and that's never changed.

It also wasn't easy for me when the tables turned and we focused on my imperfections. Dale has always said that mothers are special, and he knew I would do anything for the happiness of my children. That's what moms do: We live for our children. Developing a willingness to be told I'm wrong and a willingness to accept criticism has been and is still hard for me. Even today when I'm criticized, my initial instinct is to resist. I am, after all, imperfect. The difference today is that I know any change I make is for the benefit of my children, and I want nothing more in the world than their happiness.

In the end, if we want our children to be happy, we must never stop trying.

We have tried to assemble the pieces of our journey and the ideas that worked for us in a way that a reader can follow and apply in his or her own home. We hope we have given you a "how." So much of what we learned is common sense, but not always common practice. We hope to have provided a framework to help you improve your family, your way.

With that in mind, we would like to leave you with four final thoughts – four truths that, without an ounce of doubt, are the important lessons we've learned from our journey.

1. You Must Go First

You cannot ask your children to change if you are unwilling to change first. When they see you changing and willing to go first, they will follow your example. Put simply: Be the change you want to see in your children (taken from Gandhi's famous quote, "Be the change you want to see in the world"). If you want your child to stop doing something, you need to stop doing it first.

For most of us, change is unintentional. It's all part of our life's experiences. We change because we gain experience and knowledge throughout our lives. When it comes to family, we need to change intentionally. Intentional change is more focused and purposeful, and is easier for our kids to identify. The more intentional change we make today as individuals and parents, the better probability our family has to succeed. We are, after all, our children's most important teachers.

Be the example, and go first.

2. It Takes Time

This point was and is still Dale's hardest to accept, but he is so much better, more patient, than before. Our children are young, and who they will become is still being molded. We cannot expect them to learn at an adult level, but at times that's exactly what we do. When we parent with that kind of impatience, we are the problem. Nothing happened quickly in our home, and the sooner we accepted that, the happier we were as a family.

We all talk about how quickly life moves and how "they'll be gone before you know it," but the truth is that we do have time. Whether your child is 8 years old or 18, change takes time. Let it start today and be patient. You may not get the immediate satisfaction you are looking for, but if you are patient, positive change will come.

3. No One Does It Alone

Everyone, and we mean *everyone*, needs help. Take someone you respect and learn about him or her. You will learn that in their life and journey there were many people along the way who helped them succeed. Everyone has somebody, if not numerous people, who helped them on their journey.

We appreciate that some individuals reading this book are married and will look to their spouse to do this together, but we also understand that there are others who are single parents. You do not have to do this alone. Look to your parents, siblings, friends, support groups, whomever. If there is one thing we understand about human nature, it is that people are willing to help. Do not believe you have to travel this journey alone.

4. There Is a Story Behind Every Door

The final point is one that we've thought about and talked about many times, especially as we contemplated opening up and sharing our story. To share our story, we realized we had to be uncomfortable and tell more about our imperfect ways than we ever thought we would. Yes, sharing our story is uncomfortable, but ultimately we realized we couldn't help your family progress if we didn't.

We don't want the readers of this book to believe for a moment that we have it all figured out. Trust me, there are plenty of days we still struggle, we still argue, and we still worry about our children. As we were finalizing this book, Grant was back seeing specialists, because there were questions regarding the diagnosis of his ADHD and his continuous struggle to focus. Dominic, who had made great headway in his reading, was falling behind in math and is back in afterschool tutoring. Elizabeth has fought hard to gain her first 4.0 grade-point average (GPA) ever! However, it was not without a great deal of effort on her behalf and at times additional assistance from others with her math and reading comprehension.

We know that behind the door of every home there is a story of struggles, hardship, and ongoing challenges. In the course of writing this book, we shared our story with many people, and many of them have shared their stories with us. We have come to appreciate that there are many imperfect parents who, like us, simply want to do better for their families.

It's human nature to put our best foot forward and hide our struggles. And, in comparing one's family with other families, it is human nature to think that they are better, they do it right, they have money, they have smart kids, they have athletic kids, or that they have it made. It's simply not true, and comparing your family to others makes parenting all the more difficult.

You've heard the phrase, "keeping up with the Joneses." Well, in today's world, that sentiment has extended to parenting. In so many cases, parents are so focused on being the "cool parents" and wanting to be their children's friend that they forget that they need to be just "parents" first. Sadly, as a teacher, I see this every day, and the results are not pretty.

We do this because parenting is the most competitive sport that exists. Listen to parents in conversation. Everyone is so focused on "my kid too" stories, wanting to establish the success of their child or their family. After the conversation, many parents fret: *They've got it good. We need to do more, better, etc. for our kids. They go to better schools; they are smarter; they are better at sports.* Instead of trying to compete, stop and focus on what makes your children, you, and your family happy. Stop worrying about what you've convinced yourself you have to do to keep up with the Joneses.

Everyone has problems, EVERYONE. Everyone has a story, EVERYONE. If we care about others, if we want others to truly succeed, then we shouldn't be in competition with them, but look to support them and wish for their success, not compare and chase. For us, this mindset shift allowed us to focus where it mattered most: our family's happiness.

We hope we have inspired you to start on your own path toward being "a better me for a better we." We wish you the best of luck on your journey to building your family, your way by turning common sense into common practice.

About Dale and Monica Vernon

Dale and Monica Vernon: Two ordinary imperfect parents with 3 teenage children and a family dog from a suburb of Cleveland, Ohio. When confronted with a family crisis that threatened to destroy their family and their marriage, they put their business and teaching professional careers to work and began an experiment to find a way to succeed together as a family. The outcome was learning the power of being intentional parents who are effective by establishing, living and communicating through their values. Dale and Monica can be contacted at Dale@Imperfectparentslead.com and Monica@Imperfectparentslead.com.

55191320R00096

Made in the USA
Lexington, KY
13 September 2016